W9-BLO-355

The Cape Cod Fish & Seafood Cookbook

From Basic to Gourmet

by Gillian Drake

SHANK PAINTER PUBLISHING • CAPE COD • MASSACHUSETTS

Acknowledgments

The author wishes to thank the following people for their help with the production of this book: Maggie Barrett, Molly Benjamin, Noel Beyle, Alice Brock, Ciro Cozzi, Jarlath Hamrock, Fred Hemley, Bobbie Keane, Rena Lindstrom, Irene Lipton, Sandy McDermott, Sheila Sinead McGuinness, Major-General Leonard Phelps, and John Roderick of Seamen's Bank; and extends her appreciation to all restaurant owners, chefs, friends, and acquaintances who so generously allowed their favorite recipes to be published in this book.

Text © 1998, Gillian Drake
Illustrations © 1998, Sandy Hogan McDermott
ALL RIGHTS RESERVED
This book, or parts thereof, may not be reproduced in any form without permission in writing from the publisher.

Grateful acknowledgment is made to Parnassus Imprints, Inc., for permission to reprint recipes from the following previously published material: Excerpts from *The Provincetown Seafood Cookbook* by Howard Mitcham, © 1975 by Howard Mitcham; excerpts from *Clams, Mussels, Oysters, Scallops & Snails* by Howard Mitcham, © 1990 by Howard Mitcham. Reprinted by permission of Parnassus Imprints, Inc.

BOOK DESIGN: Gillian Drake
COVER DESIGN: Irene Lipton
ILLUSTRATIONS: Sandy Hogan McDermott
HISTORIC PHOTOGRAPHS: George Elmer Browne, courtesy of Fred Hemley
HISTORIC POSTCARDS: Courtesy of Noel Beyle

LIBRARY OF CONGRESS CATALOGING-IN-PUBLICATION DATA

Drake, Gillian.
    The Cape Cod fish & seafood cookbook : from basic to gourmet /
by Gillian Drake
    —1st ed.
    p. cm.
    Other title: The Cape Cod fish and seafood cookbook
    Includes index.
    ISBN: 1-888959-27-4

    1. Cookery (Seafood) 2. Seafood. I. Title. II. Title: The Cape Cod fish and seafood cookbook

TX747.D73 1997   641.6'92
                            QB197-40527

PUBLISHED BY:

SHANK PAINTER PUBLISHING COMPANY

P. O. Box 2001 • Provincetown • Cape Cod • MA 02657
Write for our catalogue of regional cookbooks and guide books.

ISBN 1-888959-27-4

PRINTED IN USA

Contents

DEDICATED TO MY MOTHER
BETTY PHELPS
1919-1996

In gratitude for a lifetime of culinary adventures.

Foreword

I got my first taste of fresh seafood early in my childhood at the beaches and estuaries of the Pembrokeshire coastline, now a National Park, in Southwest Wales where I was born. We would go out in great family groups crabbing and cockling, down to the vast ocean beaches of the Atlantic at low tide, twenty or so of us, with our crab hooks and shrimping nets (ever hopeful) for day-long picnics, returning home triumphant with buckets of crabs and tubs full of cockles, and the occasional oyster if we were lucky, all to be boiled up and eaten that night in a great feast. The joker of the family, Uncle Billy, would promise us sixpence per crab, half a crown for a lobster. We children would go running excitedly over the rocks hunting in the crevices for crustaceans of any persuasion, jockeying plenty of feisty crabs out of their hiding places and into a bucket—but never a lobster. It was only years later I learned that lobsters don't live in rocks, but stroll along the sandy ocean floor. Which is why we have plenty of lobsters on Cape Cod and not too many crabs worth eating.

It seemed no small coincidence that I would wash up onto the Cape in the early '70s, a refugee from Central London, thirsting for open spaces and that briny smell in the air, to be once again held in the sway of nature's rhythms—unlike London where you couldn't tell one season from the next and the shortest day was often warmer than the longest.

Seafood had always been treated as exotic fare in our family. From my years in Hong Kong in the 1950s, when our Chinese chef, Ah Chow, would cook glorious dishes of juicy Pacific prawns and lobster in sweet and sour sauce, to family holidays in Brittany and the Adriatic coast of Italy where we learned to appreciate oysters, langoustines, squid, octopus—you name it, we tried it, even winkles—fresh seafood was always the meal of choice and we felt that we dined like kings.

Later, I found I had developed a fascination for fish markets, from the jellied-eel stands and fish barrows of the East End of London to the fancy display at the food hall in Harrods, where the fishmongers artfully arranged huge creamy scallops in their shells, eels, whelks, skate, mean-looking crabs, whole salmon, eyes gleaming brightly, and rows of shimmering mackerel that looked like they had just jumped out of the water—all manner of fascinating sea creatures. But to come to Cape Cod and discover a whole new cast of characters, now that was exciting. Never before had I seen such abundant seafood—great bowls of steamer clams, platters of oysters, the sweetest scallops I had ever tasted, and the lobster, oh, the lobster! . . . as well as species of game fish I never knew existed—swordfish, striped bass, fresh tuna, mako shark, and bluefish, fresh as could be, delicious simply grilled.

However wonderful all those fish displays were, I found them a bit intimidating and if I ever cooked fish it was usually a frozen, breaded fillet of haddock or cod. It takes a little nerve to buy something you've never tasted before, let alone cooked. During the course of my twenty-five years on the Cape, I've learned to appreciate and cook all its available seafood, and this collection of recipes, gathered along the way, represents the basic methods of preparing each species . . . plus more adventurous recipes for those who don't want to face oysters on-the-half-shell or plain boiled lobster *one more time*. Some of these recipes are from the old school—before *cuisine minceur* raised its questionable head—and liberal use is made of certain ingredients that are frowned on today . . . butter, cream, salt pork . . . but, what the heck, they taste great!

Many of these recipes come from friends, and from some of the Cape's finest chefs, who also became friends, because if there's something I like better than cooking, it's eating—especially eating out, and before my daughter was born I dined out just about every night. So this is a collection of the best from the dozen cookbooks I've written or compiled, along with my personal favorites, my favorite adaptations, and those of my friends. I hope, whether you choose to be adventurous or stick to the basics, that you enjoy these seafood recipes as much as I have.

The author gathering cockles
with her mother in
Pembrokeshire, Wales, c. 1949.

Clamming in early spring at Ryder's Cove, Chatham.

Clams & Quahogs

There are few meals as tasty as a bowl of steamers, redolent with garlic, dunked in melted butter and with plenty fresh crusty bread to soak up the broth. Or succulent clams casino, baked with that naughty little piece of crispy bacon on top. Can you ever only have one? I've been known to gobble up several dozen at one sitting.

And they are fun to catch, or rather, gather—for they don't take much catching, just some digging. Nearly every town on the Cape has its shellfish beds, and permits may be obtained for as little as $10—all you then need is a rake and a bucket. The location of clam beds will vary from year to year to protect immature clams, so check with your local shellfish warden for the open beds. You'll also need a clamming gauge to measure your catch, since gathering undersized clams is illegal. Young clams must be returned to their habitat—do them a favor by poking them back into the sand to grow for another season.

There are three types of clam found on the Cape: hard-shell or quahogs, sea clams, and soft-shell clams. Hard-shell clams come in three sizes: littlenecks, cherrystones, and chowders. These are the same species of clam, their names merely relate to size. The littleneck is the smallest and most tender; the cherrystone is about twice the size of the littleneck; while chowders range from 4" long to bigger than a softball.

The larger hard-shell clams, or chowders, tend to be tougher and are usually minced for use in recipes such as chowder and clam pie. Quahogs are now widely aquacultured around the Cape, especially in Wellfleet. The farmed species is slightly different from the wild clam, identified by a distinctive pattern reminiscent of an Indian blanket, and are claimed to be meatier and sand-free.

The surf clam or sea clam lives on the exposed outer beaches of the Cape and can grow up to 8" long, sometimes even bigger. They often wash ashore after a storm and are good minced in a sea clam pie. These are the shells that often end their days as ashtrays and soapdishes. Keep an eye out for aquacultured immature surf clams which may soon be available at your fish market—called butter clams, they taste very much like steamers.

The soft-shell clams are usually referred to as steamer clams. When true Cape Codders refer to "clams" they mean steamers, while hard-shell clams are called "quahogs"—pronounced, and sometimes spelled, "cohogs." Steamers are tender, sweet and flavorful, and are most often used for steaming or frying. They are 2" to 3" in length and their thin, white, elliptical shells have rounded edges, are easily broken, and do not close tightly. The clam's foot emerges from an opening at one end, and at the other end extends its siphon, through which it feeds. When eating steamers, peel off the dark membrane from the neck of the clam. Some people prefer to bite off the tough end of the siphon.

Steamers live buried in mud or sandy tidal flats and often retain sand in their siphons. Since Cape Cod clams usually come from a sandy bed, it's best to soak them for about an hour in a bowl of water, enough to cover them, to which you may add a handful of cornmeal. Leave them in a cool place and change the water and cornmeal every so often; this will help the clams flush out any sand. Some people swear a spoonful of ground mustard added to the water will help the process. Rinse the clams alternately in warm and cold water in the kitchen sink to get rid of any exterior grit. Clams will live for days in the vegetable drawer of the refrigerator.

Steamer Clams

Simple is best for these succulent bivalves. This basic recipe can be varied by adding other ingredients, such as crumbled linguiça or bacon, chopped peppers and onion, or chopped tomatoes and basil.

SERVES 4 **AS AN** **APPETIZER**	**48 steamer clams (more for a main course)** **1 cup white wine** **1 cup water** **4 oz butter** **1/2 teaspoon freshly-ground black pepper** **2 tablespoons chopped fresh parsley**

Scrub the clams well. Do this gently as the shells are thin and brittle and crack very easily. Pour the wine and water into a large pot with a tight fitting lid and add the butter, pepper, and parsley. Carefully add the clams, cover the pot and steam for 15 or 20 minutes until all the clams have opened. Take care not to overcook them. Ladle the clams into large soup plates and serve with a cup of the broth and a cup of melted butter on the side.

To eat steamers, remove the clam from its shell, hold it by the siphon, peel back the membrane, and dip the clam first into broth (to remove the sand), then into melted butter, and then pop it into your mouth. You may bite off and discard the tough end of the siphon. Provide plenty of fresh, crusty bread to soak up the broth and accompany with chilled white wine or cold beer.

Grilled Steamers

A friend from Chatham, Chris Dawson, who seems to grill everything he catches, gave me this recipe for grilled steamers: Allow a pound of steamers for 2 people. Scrub them well and pile into the center of a large sheet of heavy-duty aluminum foil. Sprinkle with a good shake of Tabasco and toss on a tablespoon of prepared chopped garlic in oil. Wrap up the steamers in foil to make a loose parcel and grill over a very hot flame for 12 minutes. Open the parcel carefully and serve with herbed bread. Delicious!

Portuguese Steamed Littlenecks

SERVES 4

48 littleneck clams

1 lb linguica sausage

1 cup chopped fresh tomatoes

1 onion, finely chopped

1/4 cup chopped scallions

2 tablespoons fresh parsley, chopped

2 cloves garlic, crushed

1 cup white wine

Scrub clams well and rinse in cool water. Slice linguica and crumble. Place linguica, tomatoes, onion, scallions, parsley, garlic, wine and 3/4 cup of water into a large kettle. Place clams on top, cover, and bring to a boil. Boil until the clams have opened completely. To serve, divide clams and sauce equally into 4 large soup plates. Serve with extra broth on the side and plenty of crusty Portuguese bread.

This recipe may easily be transformed into Steamed Clams Madeira by omitting the linguica and replacing the white wine with Madeira and the parsley for fresh chopped basil.

Clams Casino

SERVES 4

24 littleneck or cherrystone clams
1 teaspoon chopped garlic
2 tablespoons chopped onion
2 tablespoons butter
dash of Tabasco sauce
1 cup bread crumbs
4 slices bacon

Sauté garlic and onion in butter over low heat. Add bread crumbs and Tabasco and mix thoroughly. Open the clams and top with bread crumb mixture. Cut each slice of bacon into six pieces and place small slices of bacon on top of each clam. Bake clams in the oven on a cookie sheet at 450 degrees until bacon browns.

Clam diggers in Provincetown, c. 1920.   POSTCARD COURTESY OF NOEL W. BEYLE

Aesop's Clam Chowder

The origin of the term "chowder" comes from the French "chaudiere," a large cauldron in which fishermen in rural France cook various fish soups and stews. A Cape Cod clam chowder is distinguished by the addition of milk or cream. This gourmet version of clam chowder comes from Aesop's Tables, a fine restaurant located in a magnificent former sea captain and governor's mansion in Wellfleet.

SERVES 4

1 lb fresh littleneck clams

1 cup white wine

2 potatoes, steamed, skinned and diced

4 strips bacon

5 stalks celery, finely chopped

2 carrots, finely chopped

1 large white Spanish onion, finely chopped

1/2 cup butter

3 tablespoons flour

1/2 cup light cream

dash of Tabasco

salt and pepper to taste

dash of Worcestershire sauce

Scrub the clams and steam them in 2 cups of water and a cup of white wine in a pot with a tight fitting lid. Steam for about 5 minutes or until the clams open. Remove clams from the pot and reserve the broth. Chop the clams when they have cooled. Sauté the bacon, leaving the drippings in the pan. Add the celery, carrots, and onion to pan and sauté for 20 minutes over medium heat. Add 3 cups of the clam broth and simmer for half an hour.

Meanwhile, in a small pan make a roux with 1/2 cup of butter and 3 tablespoons of flour. Stir the roux into the broth/vegetables mixture to thicken. Add the cream, diced potatoes, and the chopped clams. Heat through but do not boil. Season to taste with a dash of Tabasco, salt, pepper, and Worcestershire sauce, and serve.

Traditional Cape Cod Clam Chowder

SERVES 10

2 cups chopped quahogs

4 cups thinly-sliced peeled potatoes

1 large onion, sliced thin

1 cup finely-diced salt pork

4 cups scalded milk

cream, butter and flour to taste

salt and pepper to taste

Scrub clams well and wash thoroughly. Place them in a large pot with a tight-fitting lid and pour in a cup of water. Steam the clams until they open. Remove clam meats from their shells and strain the clam liquor. You may chop the clams by hand or coarsely grind them in an old hand grinder, reserving any clam juice.

Simmer the potatoes until cooked but still firm. Fry out the salt pork in a large, heavy pot until crisp. Add the chopped onions and sauté for 5 minutes until lightly brown. Add the hard parts of the chopped clams and pour on $2^1/_2$ cups of boiling water. Cook for 3 minutes but do not boil. Season to taste. Stir in 4 cups of scalded milk. Heat the clam liquor and add to the chowder along with the soft parts of the clams and any clam juice. Thicken to taste with a little roux (one tablespoon each melted butter and flour cooked together). Stir in a little cream to taste before serving and top with a sprinkling of paprika and a knob of butter as a final touch.

Chowder tastes even better the next day when the flavors have blended, but be sure to reheat it gently and don't allow it to boil. Clam chowder freezes well. Cooking the potatoes in clam liquor adds to the flavor. Try allspice, sage, or mace as a seasoning—some people like to add fresh rosemary for a different flavor.

Italian-Style Baked Stuffed Clams

SERVES 4

24 quahogs

2 tablespoons olive oil

2 cloves garlic, crushed

3 scallions

1½ cups bread crumbs

1/2 cup tomato sauce, preferably homemade

1/2 cup Parmesan cheese

1 teaspoon chopped basil

1 teaspoon chopped oregano

Scrub clams and steam in a small amount of water until shells just open. Remove clams and leave to cool. When cool, open clams, remove meats, and discard top shells. Chop clams and set aside.

Chop scallions finely. Heat oil in a pan and sauté garlic and scallions until translucent. Blend in bread crumbs, seasonings, tomato sauce and Parmesan cheese. Mix in chopped clams and stuff shells with this mixture. Sprinkle each stuffed clam with a few drops of olive oil and a little Parmesan cheese. Bake in oven for 15 minutes at 400 degrees, or until tops brown. Serve at once.

Baked Stuffed Quahogs

AMEIJOAS ASSARDE COM RECHEIO

This recipe is from TRADITIONAL PORTUGUESE RECIPES FROM PROVINCETOWN *by Mary Alice Luiz Cook, who was born in Olhao, Portugal, in 1914.*

SERVES 4 - 6

12 or more large quahogs (save the shells)
1/2 cup chopped onion
1 lb mushrooms, sliced
3 tablespoons butter for topping and frying
2 tablespoons flour
1 teaspoon salt
1/2 teaspoon black pepper
1 cup fresh bread crumbs
1/2 cup melted butter

Wash the clams well to remove any grit Steam them in just enough water to cover. Remove clams and grind the meats, reserving the shells

Sauté chopped onion and mushrooms in 2 tablespoons of butter until soft. Blend in the flour and seasonings, stirring well. Stir in the ground clams and any clam liquor, and cook the mixture gently until it thickens a little. Set aside.

Mix the bread crumbs with 1/2 cup of melted butter. Butter the clam shells and fill with clam mixture. Top with bread crumbs, sprinkle with paprika, and dot with butter.

Bake in a hot oven at 400 degrees for 10 minutes or until lightly browned.

This is a very filling but tasty dish. We usually served it as an appetizer or at parties.

Spaghetti Con Vongole
SPAGHETTI WITH WHITE CLAM SAUCE

Here is my own favorite recipe for this delectable classic Italian dish from the Adriatic coast of Italy, which adapts perfectly to our native clams.

SERVES 4

48 cherrystone clams

1/2 cup virgin olive oil

1 oz butter

6 cloves garlic, finely chopped

4 scallions, finely sliced, white and green parts

1 tablespoon chopped fresh basil leaves

1/2 teaspoon hot red pepper flakes, or to taste

1/4 cup finely chopped pine nuts

2 tablespoons chopped fresh parsley

1 lb spaghetti

Open the clams and cut each clam into thirds or quarters. Reserve the clam juice. Cook the pasta in salted boiling water until al dente.

Prepare the sauce while the spaghetti is cooking. Heat the oil and butter in a skillet, add the chopped garlic and sauté for a few minutes. Do not let the garlic brown. Add the scallions and sauté for a few minutes. Add the clam juice, basil, and red pepper and heat to boiling. Turn down the heat and add the chopped clams, pine nuts and half of the chopped parsley. Cook over low to moderate heat for a few minutes until the clams are heated through—they will turn white. Be careful not to overcook the clams or they will be tough.

Drain the spaghetti when cooked and transfer it to a warm serving bowl. Pour the clam sauce over the spaghetti and toss together. Serve immediately, sprinkled with chopped parsley and plenty of freshly-grated Parmesan cheese.

Pasta with Red Clam Sauce

SERVES 6

72 cherrystone clams
4 cloves garlic, finely minced
1 oz butter
1/4 cup olive oil
1/2 cup diced onion
1 28-oz can diced plum tomatoes
2 tablespoons chopped parsley
1 teaspoon chopped fresh oregano
1/2 teaspoon dried thyme
1/4 teaspoon crushed red pepper flakes
1/2 cup dry red wine
salt to taste
1½ lbs pasta, cooked

Shuck the clams over a pan to catch the juice. Grind the clams in an old-fashioned grinder. If you don't have one, the clams can be minced in a food processor, but take care not to grind them too finely.

Heat the olive oil and butter in a skillet and sauté the onion, garlic and oregano lightly. Add the clam juice, wine, tomatoes, parsley, thyme, salt, and red pepper flakes. Simmer the sauce uncovered for an hour, stirring occasionally. Add the minced clams and cook gently for 5 minutes. To serve, spoon over cooked pasta of your choice and serve piping hot in warmed soup plates. Garnish with chopped parsley and freshly grated Parmesan cheese.

Pasta with Clams Meridionale

36 cherrystone clams

5 quarts water

1½ cups reserved clam juice (add bottled if
   necessary to make up amount)

salt to taste if desired

6 tablespoons olive oil

1/2 cup heavy cream

1 tablespoon finely minced garlic

1/3 cup finely chopped parsley

2 tablespoons butter, cut into small pieces

1 tablespoon Pernod or Ricard

1 lb spaghetti

Shuck the clams over a bowl to catch as much juice as possible. Strain and reserve the clam juice in a measuring cup. Make this amount up to 1½ cups with bottled clam juice if necessary. Place the clams on a flat surface and chop them finely. Bring the water to a boil and add half a cup of the clam juice and salt to taste if desired. Add the spaghetti and cook until al dente.

Pour the remaining clam juice into large skillet or casserole sitting over very low heat. Drain the cooked spaghetti and add it to the clam juice. Add the cream and stir. Let the mixture heat slowly while the sauce is being prepared.

Heat oil in a small skillet. Add the chopped clams, garlic, and parsley and heat for about a minute or until thoroughly hot, but do not cook. Pour this sauce over the spaghetti, then toss in the butter. Add the Pernod or Ricard and toss the spaghetti again. Serve immediately.

Pauli's Pasta with Clams

This is simple but delicious—thanks to Karen Gunderson for sharing her favorite clam recipe with me.

SERVES 4

36 littleneck clams, well scrubbed
3 Vidalia onions, thinly sliced
1/4 lb butter
2 cloves garlic, crushed
1/2 cup white wine or
 juice from 1 lemon (or 2 if you
 prefer more lemon flavor)
1 lb linguine

Melt the butter in a pot and sauté the onions and garlic until the onions are translucent and just start to turn brown. Add the scrubbed clams with the wine or lemon juice and cover the pot with a tight-fitting lid. Steam clams over medium-high heat. Check the clams occasionally and take them out with tongs as they open. Place them on a platter and keep warm. Continue steaming the clams until they are all open.

Meanwhile, cook the linguine al dente and strain. Pour the pasta into the pot with the clam liquor and toss well. Serve the linguine with sauce in pasta bowls and place the platter of steamed clams in the center of the table.

Cape Cod Clam Casserole

SERVES 4

24 littleneck clams, well scrubbed

2 eggs, slightly beaten

2 cups cream sauce

4 oz mushrooms

1/2 cup butter, melted

about 2 dozen crushed soda crackers

Place washed clams in a saucepan with a tight-fitting lid in one cup of water. Steam until all clams have opened and remove from heat. Discard any clams that do not open. Separate clams from shells, discard shells, strain juice and reserve.

Chop the mushrooms and sauté for a few minutes in a little butter. Mix together the eggs, cream sauce, butter, mushrooms, clam broth and enough soda crackers to thicken sauce slightly. Coarsely chop the clams and add them to the mixture. Place in a shallow, greased casserole and bake uncovered at 350 degrees for an hour.

Clam Quiche

18 cherrystone clams
6 slices bacon
1 small onion, chopped
4 eggs
1 cup light cream
1 cup clam juice
1 9-inch pie crust, unbaked
salt and pepper to taste

Shuck clams and reserve clam juice. Wash the clams and chop finely. Sauté bacon until crisp. Remove bacon from skillet and drain on paper towels. In the same skillet, sauté the chopped onion in bacon fat until transparent.

Crumble the bacon and sprinkle over the bottom of the pie shell. Add clams and onion to the pie shell. Beat together the eggs, cream, and one cup of strained clam juice. Season with salt and pepper to taste. Pour egg mixture over clams and bake in oven at 375 degrees for 40 minutes.

Clam Fritters

48 cherrystone clams

1½ cups flour

1 teaspoon baking powder

2 eggs, beaten lightly

1 cup half-and-half

1 medium onion, diced

1/4 teaspoon ground cumin

2 cloves garlic, minced

1 teaspoon salt

1/4 teaspoon freshly ground black pepper

1/4 teaspoon crushed red pepper seeds

Shuck or steam open the fresh clams, reserving the liquor. Chop the meats finely.

In a bowl mix the flour, baking powder, onion, cumin, garlic, salt and peppers. Add the eggs and the chopped clams and mix well. Add the half-and-half with enough clam liquor to make a thick batter.

Pour oil into a skillet to a depth of about 1/2 inch. Drop teaspoonsful of batter into the hot oil and sauté until golden brown on all sides. Drain on paper towels and serve while hot.

NOTE: Finely chopped linguica added to the batter creates spicy Portuguese clam fritters.

Scalloped Clams

2 cups minced clam meat, about 24 quahogs

1/2 onion, finely chopped

1/4 cup chopped parsley

1 teaspoon salt

dash of Tabasco sauce

1/2 cup bread crumbs

1 cup coarse cracker crumbs

1/2 cup melted butter

1/2 cup heavy cream

In a bowl, mix together the chopped onion, minced clams, chopped parsley, salt, and a dash of Tabasco. In a separate bowl, mix the bread and cracker crumbs with the melted butter. Set aside a third of the mixture. Combine remaining crumb mixture with the clams and spoon into a buttered baking dish. Top with remaining crumbs, dot with butter, and pour heavy cream over the top. Bake for 25 minutes in the oven at 375 degrees.

Quahog Pie

This is a traditional Cape Cod favorite.

SERVES 4 TO 6

Preheat oven
to 350
degrees

24 cherrystone clams

6 tablespoons butter

1 medium potato, diced

2 medium onions, diced

4 tablespoons diced salt pork

1/4 cup finely chopped celery

2 tablespoons diced red pepper

2 tablespoons chopped parsley

1/2 cup heavy cream

dash of cayenne pepper

1 oz brandy

salt and freshly ground black pepper to taste

pastry for a 2-crust, 10-inch pie

Shuck or steam open the clams and chop them coarsely, saving 1/2 cup of liquor. Melt 4 tablespoons of butter in a skillet and add the onions, celery and salt pork. Cook until the vegetables are soft and the pork is opaque white. Add the diced red pepper, potatoes, parsley, and chopped quahogs and sauté for 5 minutes, stirring constantly. Place in a bowl and set aside. Melt 2 tablespoons of butter in a skillet and stir in 2 tablespoons of flour. Add the clam liquor and stir until the mixture is smooth and slightly thickened. Stir in the brandy and then add the cream slowly, stirring until the mixture is smooth. Add the cayenne and black pepper, and salt if needed. Stir the clam mixture into this sauce and mix well. Line a 10" pie pan with pastry and pour the clam mixture into it. Cover with a pastry top and seal the edges with a fork. Brush with milk and punch a few small holes in the top to allow steam to escape. Bake in the oven for 30 minutes or until the top is nicely browned.

Quahogs with Rice

Linguiça sausage adds spice to this tasty recipe from Traditional Portuguese Recipes from Provincetown *by Mary Alice Luiz Cook.*

SERVES 4

24 or more small quahogs
1 cup white wine
1/4 lb salt pork cut up in small pieces
1 onion, sliced
2 cloves garlic, minced
1/2 cup chopped parsley
4 oz linguiça sausage, crumbled
freshly-ground black pepper
juice of 1/2 lemon
1¹/₂ cups rice
1/4 lb butter

Wash clams well to remove any grit. Place clams in a heavy pot with a tight fitting lid and steam them in 1/2 cup white wine and 1/2 cup water. Steam until the shells open (discard any which do not open), strain the liquor, and set aside.

In another pan, fry out the pork, add the sliced onion and garlic and sauté slowly until translucent. Add the linguiça and sauté for a few minutes. Add the strained clam liquor and the clams in their shells, and add the lemon juice. Stir in the rice and cook slowly in the clam liquor, stirring often until the rice is golden yellow but not browned. You may need to add a little more water from time to time.

When the rice is cooked, stir in the butter and parsley and season with black pepper. Turn off the heat and let the rice stand for about 5 minutes before serving.

For a change, you may like to substitute cornmeal for the rice, though it will take a little longer to cook.

Fishing boat moored in Rock Harbor, Orleans.

Mussels

Mussels were sadly neglected in this region until recently, probably because the Cape is known as clam country. In Europe, the mussel has long been considered a delicacy, but this mollusc has grown enormously in popularity here in recent years.

The edible mussel commonly found in local waters is the blue mussel, which grows up to 4" long. Mussels can be found in small clusters or in vast beds. They attach themselves to pilings or rocks with strands called byssus threads, or "beards." These tough threads enable mussels to cling to virtually any surface, even in pounding surf. Mussels grow rapidly and reach harvestable size in two years. No other shellfish is more nutritious than the mussel—it has a high proportion of meat to shell, and is one of the most abundant meats in the world.

Harvesting mussels requires no fancy equipment, just a pair of eager hands and a container. Choose mussels that are uncovered only at very low tide (the farther out one goes the bigger and better mussels become) and that grow in moving water or tidal channels. If you intend to store your catch for a few days, take entire clumps of mussels so that the threads remain intact—the mussels will stay fresher longer. Store them in the refrigerator covered with a wet cloth.

Before you cook mussels, remove any with broken shells and squeeze each mussel firmly between thumb and forefinger to make sure the shells are locked, signifying the mussel is alive. Some shells may be full of mud—a "mudder" will ruin a recipe, so the squeeze test is important. Remove the beards with a sharp knife, scrub the shells well, and wash them in water several times until the final washing water is free from grit. To save yourself this chore, aquacultured mussels are now widely available, cleaned and debearded and ready to go.

The simplest, and many believe the most delicious, way to cook mussels is to steam them in a large pan with a glass of dry white wine, a crushed clove of garlic, and a handful of chopped parsley. Cover the pan with a tight-fitting lid and steam over high heat until all the mussels open, about 5 to 10 minutes. Ladle into soup plates and serve with plenty of crusty fresh bread to mop up the broth. Provide a large bowl for the empty shells, and serve with a bottle of chilled white wine. This simple method works especially well with the small and tender mussels available for the taking all around the coast of Cape Cod.

Some people like to strain the broth, but it's not necessary—any sediment will sink to the bottom of the cup. A fun way to eat steamed mussels is the way the French do in Brittany—select an empty pair of hinged mussel shells to use as tweezers to remove the mussel meats from their shells and pop them directly into your mouth after dunking in broth.

A piquant variation of the classic steamed mussels, or *moules marinière*, is Portuguese Mussels—simply add some crumbled linguiça (a spicy hard sausage) and a handful of finely-chopped green pepper to the pot before steaming and serve with fresh Portuguese rolls (widely available on the Cape) and a bottle of chilled vinho verde, a refreshing Portuguese white wine.

Mussel Soup

SERVES 8

2 quarts mussels

1/2 cup dry white wine

2 cloves garlic, crushed

2 medium onions, finely chopped

2 tablespoons chopped parsley

3 oz butter

3 cups boiling water

pinch of bouquet garni

1/2 cup hot milk

2 egg yolks

1/2 cup cream

juice of 1 lemon

8 small pieces toasted French bread

salt and pepper to taste

Scrub mussels thoroughly and remove the beards. Steam the mussels open in 1/2 cup of white wine with a clove of crushed garlic. Strain the broth and set aside. Sauté the chopped onions and a clove of crushed garlic in butter in a saucepan. When the onions are translucent, add the strained mussel broth, bouquet garni, chopped parsley, 3 cups of boiling water, and 1/2 cup of hot milk. Simmer gently for 15 minutes. Add the shelled mussels and simmer for a few more minutes. Season to taste.

Beat the egg yolks and cream in a large bowl or soup tureen. Carefully add the lemon juice, stirring it in little by little. Pour the mussel soup over the egg and cream mixture, stirring well. Serve with toasted French bread as a garnish.

Drunken Mussels

This easy-to-prepare recipe is from the Impudent Oyster in Chatham.

SERVES 6
AS AN
APPETIZER

5 dozen mussels

1 cup water

1 cup tamari

1½ cups saki

1 cup sugar

1 oz fresh grated ginger

1 tablespoon ground Szechuan peppers

Scrub the mussels thoroughly and remove beards. Steam mussels in a cup of water in a covered pot until they open. Remove mussels from their liquor with a slotted spoon. Remove mussel meats from their shells and set aside. Return pot containing stock to stove-top and reduce liquid to one level cup.

Add remaining ingredients to reduced mussel liquor and mix in well. Toss mussels in liquor, transfer to a covered container, and let stand overnight. Remove mussels with a slotted spoon and serve with sauce on the side. Garnish with grated daikon and wasabi (Japanese horse-radish).

Mussel Fritters

1 pint mussel meats

1 onion

1 egg, lightly beaten

pinch of thyme

2 drops Tabasco sauce

1 tablespoon parsley, chopped fine

1/2 cup flour

1 teaspoon baking powder

Grind mussels and onion together in a grinder. Mix in beaten egg, chopped parsley, thyme, and Tabasco. Add flour and baking powder and mix in well. Drop spoonfuls of the fritter batter into hot oil and fry briefly until golden brown. Serve with tartar sauce.

Midia Dolma

This recipe for stuffed mussels is a classic dish from Turkey. Preparation can be time-consuming, but the end result is well worth the effort.

SERVES 6

60 plump mussels, scrubbed, with beards removed

1/2 cup olive oil

3 medium onions, chopped

1 cup uncooked long-grain rice

3 cloves garlic, crushed

1/4 cup pine nuts

1/4 cup dried currants

salt and freshly ground black pepper to taste

1/2 teaspoon ground allspice

1/2 cup chopped parsley

1 pint dry white wine

2 cups mussel broth

Place the mussels in a large pot with one cup of white wine, one chopped onion, one crushed garlic clove, and a 1/4 cup of chopped parsley. Cover and steam until the mussels open. Remove the mussels and reserve the broth. Measure the broth, and add enough water to make 2 cups. Add salt to taste.

Cook the remaining onions in olive oil over low heat until soft and translucent, about 10 minutes. Add the rice, currants, pine nuts, salt and pepper, allspice, and 1/4 cup parsley. Add the mussel broth, cover, and cook slowly until the rice has cooked and the juice has been absorbed, about 15 minutes. Add more oil or wine if the mixture seems too dry. Stuff this mixture into each mussel with your hands, making sure the 2 halves of each shell stay fixed together. Close the stuffed mussel shells (you may want to tie each mussel shut with a piece of string if you are trying to impress your guests), and layer them in a deep, wide pan or Dutch oven with a close-fitting lid.

Pour the remaining white wine into the pan, cover, and steam very gently for 30 or 40 minutes, adding more liquid if necessary. Remove from the heat and let the mussels cool.

Take the mussels out of the pot and put the mussels that were on top back into the pot so they will marinate in the liquor. After about 45 minutes, remove all the mussels and refrigerate overnight. To serve, arrange on a large platter and garnish with lemon wedges.

Mussels Stuffed with Crabmeat

SERVES 4

2 dozen mussels

2 tablespoons butter

1/2 cup crabmeat, shredded

1/2 cup mushrooms, finely minced

1 clove garlic, minced

1/4 cup minced onion

1 teaspoon lemon juice

1 tablespoon chopped parsley

dash of dried thyme

dash of cayenne pepper

salt to taste

1 tablespoon sherry

3 tablespoons bread crumbs

Scrub mussels well and remove beards. Steam in a large pot in half a cup of water until just open. Remove pot from heat and allow mussels to cool. When cool, remove top shell of each mussel.

Meanwhile, melt butter in a pan and sauté crabmeat, mushrooms, garlic, and onion until tender, but not brown. Add lemon juice, thyme, cayenne pepper, parsley, and sherry, and then season to taste. Simmer for two minutes and mix in bread crumbs.

Stuff mussel halves with crabmeat mixture and broil until light brown.

Mussels Dijon

This award-winning recipe was created by Robert Gold, chef-owner of Penguins SeaGrill in Hyannis.

SERVES 6

5 lbs mussels, scrubbed, beards removed

1 carrot, grated

1 clove garlic, chopped finely

2 scallions, diced

1/2 leek stalk, diced

2 oz olive oil

4 heaping tablespoons Grey Poupon mustard

1 pint heavy cream

1/2 pint white wine

Place grated carrot, leek, garlic, and scallions in a 4 quart pot and sauté lightly in olive oil. Add the mustard, mussels (in their shells), cream and wine and stir to mix. Cover pot and shake to make sure mussels are coated. Steam on high heat until mussels open. Cook for two minutes longer. Spoon into individual soup plates and serve with hot crusty bread.

Mussels Marinara with Tarragon

This flavorful mussel recipe comes from the Wequassett Inn in Harwich.

SERVES 2

24 mussels
1 tablespoon olive oil
2 small cloves garlic, minced
1 small shallot, finely chopped
1/4 cup red wine
1 tablespoon fresh chopped tarragon

MARINARA SAUCE:
3-4 cloves garlic, minced
1 tablespoon olive oil
1 cup crushed tomatoes with juice
1/2 small onion, diced
1 tablespoon fresh basil
2 tablespoons red wine
salt and pepper to taste

To prepare the marinara sauce, sauté the garlic and onions in olive oil. Add the red wine and cook until the ingredients are nearly dry. Add tomato, basil, salt and pepper. Cook, stirring occasionally, for 15 to 20 minutes.

Heat a tablespoon of olive oil in a large pot and sauté the garlic and shallot for a few minutes. Add the mussels, 1/4 cup of red wine, and approximately one cup of marinara sauce. Cover the pot tightly and cook until the mussels open, approximately 5 or 10 minutes. Remove the cover and stir in the chopped tarragon. Spoon the mussels and a generous quantity of broth into individual soup plates and serve with plenty of fresh crusty bread.

Mussels Orleans

This unique recipe was gleaned many years ago from the pages of the
CAPE CODDER, *hometown newspaper for Orleans and vicinity.*

SERVES 4

2 or 3 quarts mussels

1 cup white wine

3 or 4 lbs fresh spinach

4 tablespoons olive oil

3 tablespoons butter

1 cup heavy cream

4 egg yolks

pinch of saffron

3/4 cup fresh white bread crumbs

Scrub mussels and remove beards. Place in a large pot with white wine and steam until open, discarding any mussels that don't open. Strain and reserve liquid. When cool, remove mussel meats from shells.

Clean spinach well, blanch for 3 minutes, drain well, and chop. Heat spinach in a sauté pan in olive oil and butter. Season with salt and pepper. Place in a gratin dish and top with shelled mussels.

Prepare a sauce by cooking together 1/2 cup of mussel liquid, 1 cup of heavy cream, and 4 lightly beaten egg yolks over low heat until thickened. Heat gently, stirring all the time; do not boil or the eggs will curdle. Season with salt and pepper to taste and a pinch of saffron. Pour sauce over mussels, top with bread crumbs, and cook in oven at 400 degrees for about 10 minutes or until bread crumbs have browned on top.

Traditional One Pot Mussel or Clam Bake

SERVES 6 | **6 ears fresh corn**
6 small onions
6 medium-sized potatoes
3 quarts mussels or soft-shell clams
6 chicken legs
12 link sausages or 1 lb linguica,
cut into 1" pieces
1/2 bottle dry white wine, or water

Shuck the corn, peel the onions, and scrub the potatoes. Scrub the mussels well, removing the beards. Place all the ingredients, except the corn, in a large pot (no smaller than two gallons) with a well-fitting lid, in the order in which they are listed above. Cover and steam over low heat for 35 minutes. Then add the corn and steam for another 10 minutes. Test the chicken to make sure it is cooked. Serve in large soup bowls with plenty of crusty bread to soak up the broth.

Mussels & Artichokes with Pasta

This recipe is courtesy of Necee Regis, a summer resident of Wellfleet and proprietor of Necee Regis Catering in Cambridge, MA, and Miami Beach, Florida.

SERVES 2-4,
DEPENDING ON
INDIVIDUAL
APPETITES

3 dozen mussels, well scrubbed, beards removed

1¹/₂ cups white wine

1 garlic clove, crushed

10 sprigs parsley

1/2 cup sun-dried tomatoes, sliced into strips

SAUCE:

1/3 cup virgin olive oil

1 or 2 cloves garlic, crushed

1 cup chopped onion

1/2 cup fresh parsley, chopped

1 can artichoke hearts, drained, lightly chopped

3 tablespoons fresh basil, chopped

1/2 teaspoon dried oregano

2 tablespoons extra virgin olive oil

Place mussels in a saucepan with the white wine, garlic, and whole parsley sprigs. Bring to a boil, then simmer until the mussels open. Strain them and save the broth. Remove the meats from mussel shells and reserve. Place the tomatoes in the mussel broth and set aside. If the tomatoes seem very salty, rinse them in hot water first.

To make the sauce, heat 1/3 cup of olive oil in a sauté pan. Add garlic and chopped onions and sauté over low heat for about 10 minutes. Add the chopped parsley, artichoke hearts, basil, oregano, and 2 tablespoons extra virgin olive oil. Stir until heated, about 2 or 3 minutes. Add the tomatoes in mussel broth. Bring to a boil and simmer for 10 minutes. Just before serving, add the mussels and simmer to heat through, but do not overcook. Season to taste, and ladle over pasta of your choice.

Curried Mussels & Scallops

SERVES 8

**48 large mussels, well-scrubbed (or allow 8 to 10
   per person if mussels are small)**

32 sea scallops, cut into bite-sized pieces

3 tablespoons olive oil

2 cloves garlic, crushed

pinch of rosemary

pinch of black pepper

1 tablespoon chopped parsley

1/4 cup white wine

CURRY SAUCE:

2/3 cup grated coconut or ground almonds

1 cup milk

2 onions, chopped

1 apple, cored but unpeeled, and chopped

2 tomatoes, peeled, deseeded and chopped

4 tablespoons butter

2 tablespoons curry powder

salt to taste

dash of cayenne pepper

1 cup dry sherry

1 cup mussel liquor

1 cup heavy cream

Heat oil in a large pot with a tight-fitting lid and sauté the garlic until soft.
Add the mussels, rosemary, black pepper, chopped parsley, and white
wine; stir together. Cover the pot and steam for approximately five
minutes. Add the scallops and continue cooking for a few more minutes

until mussels open. Be careful not to overcook the scallops. Remove the shellfish from the pot, separate the mussel meats from their shells, and set aside. Strain liquid and reserve to make sauce.

Soak the grated coconut or ground almonds in a cup of milk while preparing the sauce.

Chop the onions, apples, and tomatoes. Melt the butter in a skillet and cook onions until glazed. Add apples, tomatoes, curry powder, and salt to taste. Add a dash of cayenne pepper if desired. Cook slowly until vegetables are tender. Add a cup of dry sherry and a cup of mussel liquor and reduce to half. Then add the soaked grated coconut (or ground almonds) and simmer for 15 minutes. Force the sauce through a fine sieve, return to stove, and add cream. Cook down for approximately 15 minutes. Adjust seasoning to taste. Add the scallops and mussel meats to the curry sauce and simmer gently for 5 minutes to heat through. Serve with Basmati rice.

New England Casserole with Cranberries

This recipe came from the CAPE CODDER *newspaper nearly 20 years ago. It sounds intriguing, but I must confess to never actually having made it. I would love to hear from anyone who has!*

SERVES 4

2 quarts mussels, well scrubbed

1 cup white wine

1 cup jellied cranberry sauce

1/4 cup butter

1/2 lb fresh mushrooms, sliced

1 medium onion, chopped

1/3 cup celery, chopped

1/4 cup flour

1 cup heavy cream

2 cups cracker crumbs

1/2 cup shredded Gruyere cheese

Scrub mussels well and remove beards. Steam mussels in wine until they open. Discard shells, reserve broth and strain. Put mussels in a buttered 2-quart baking dish. Cover with cranberry sauce. In a pan, melt butter, add mushrooms, onions, and celery, and sauté until tender. Stir in flour to coat vegetables, then stir in one cup of the reserved mussel broth with the cream. Heat, stirring constantly, until thick. Pour sauce over mussels and cranberry sauce. Top with a mixture of cracker crumbs and cheese. Bake, uncovered, in an oven at 375 degrees for about 30 minutes, or until hot and browned on top.

Pickled Mussels

This is the traditional way of serving cockles and mussels back in the old country —Olde England, that is. Thin-sliced buttered brown bread is always served as an accompaniment.

SERVES 6

3 lbs mussels

1/2 cup chopped parsley

1 onion, minced

1 garlic clove

1/2 cup olive oil

1/3 cup wine vinegar

1 bay leaf

a few drops of Tabasco

white pepper to taste

Scrub the mussels well, remove their beards, and steam in a large pot with a tightly-fitting lid. Steam until their shells open. Remove the mussel meats from their shells and place in a non-metal bowl. Add the chopped parsley, onion and the whole garlic clove. Mix together the oil, vinegar, bay leaf, Tabasco, and white pepper; pour over the mussels. Leave overnight, tossing the mixture now and then. Remove garlic clove and drain before serving.

Oyster boats and sets at Cotuit Harbor.

Oysters

O ysters are consumed joyously the world over. In Europe, oysters have been prized throughout history, and because of their reputation as an aphrodisiac (now thought to be due to their high zinc content), oysters and champagne became known as the food of lovers—Casanova reportedly consumed 50 a day to keep up his strength.

Meanwhile, across the Atlantic, the oyster was enjoyed from earliest times by native Americans, and the quality and plumpness of Wellfleet oysters was remarked upon by the Pilgrims. In 1606, the French explorer Champlain and his men gorged themselves on Wellfleet oysters when they landed at Billingsgate Island, calling their port of entry there "Oyster Harbor." Many early coastal pioneers filled their circular cellars with oysters to tide their families through harsh winters when no other form of protein was available. In the late 1800s, oysters were wildly popular and available almost everywhere in America. Shipped by train, barrels and barrels of fine Wellfleet oysters were consumed by gold miners and railroad barons in such places as Denver and Butte.

There are four major species of oyster—American, Pacific, European flat or Belon, and Olympia. Most oysters found along the East Coast are the American oyster, while West Coast oysters are largely Pacifics. The Olympia, the only one native to the West Coast, is a tiny oyster related to the European flat. The European flat is the most sought-after oyster in Europe, but they are skinny and flavorless—metallic-tasting, many say—compared to the plump Americans which are so plentiful on the Cape.

Oysters spawn prolifically and are widely aquacultured on the Cape, from Provincetown to Cotuit, often by using special collectors to collect wild spat. The tiny oysters are then moved to a sheltered environment and left to grow to marketable size in the shallows, washed by the clean cold waters of the Atlantic Ocean.

Most people are familiar with the adage that we should not eat oysters when there is no "R" in the month. One reason for this was probably a matter of safety, in that raw shellfish was less likely to be contaminated in cooler weather in the days before refrigeration. Nowadays, if oysters are properly harvested, inspected, and stored, there should be no problem with eating them in the summer season. Others reasons may be that most oysters spawn in the summer months, and spawn in oysters can be milky and unattractive. Also, they tend to be watery and a little less tasty after spawning. To confuse things further, some oysters don't spawn during the summer, and some seafood connoisseurs prefer their oysters in a prespawning state . . . but a more important point to bear in mind is that all shellfish are plumper in winter than in summer.

In the shell, oysters will stay fresh in the bottom of a refrigerator for two weeks if covered with a damp cloth to keep them moist. When kept out of the water for long, the liquid inside the shell dries up and oysters lose their flavor, so store them carefully, concave side down, so they are awash in liquid inside their shells. Before you open oysters, wash off any mud and chill them in the refrigerator, or on ice.

The thought of opening oysters can make a grown man blanch, though Julia Child pops them open using a beer can opener with no trouble. She lays the oyster flat, concave side down, and inserts the point of the opener between the shells at the hinged end, pressing on the other end until the shells are forced apart. A knife blade worked around the edges of the oyster to sever the muscle from the upper and lower shells completes the job. Or a short, stout knife will do just fine—oyster knives are readily available at most hardware stores on the Cape. Spend the money to get a good one—they're worth it.

Always wear thick, protective gloves to prevent accidents: hold the oyster rounded side down on a cutting board with your left hand and push the knife blade or pointed implement between the shells at the hinged end and pry the blade up. Then loosen the oyster in its shell by severing the adductor muscle, being careful not to spill any juice. Have patience, it takes practice to get the hang of it. When you do, keep quiet about it or you'll be rounded up for wrist-wrenching, oyster-opening duty at all your friends' cocktail parties.

If this hand method sounds too vigorous or dangerous, you can always pop the oysters in a hot oven or in hot water for a few minutes so the shell muscles relax, making opening them much easier. Or place them in the freezer for 15 minutes. Even a few seconds in the microwave does the trick. They may also be grilled—self opening, and delicious!

Once opened, the entire oyster—juice and all—should be consumed, preferably raw and chewed with relish. (I was taught as a child in Europe to swallow oysters whole, which simply gave me a mouthful of salt water and grit. I never realized what an oyster *tasted* like until I landed in America.)

The following recipes, which range from simple to gourmet, will tempt those who've become jaded with mere oysters-on-the-half-shell. Remember that however you prepare oysters, you must be vigilant not to overcook them, otherwise they will toughen and become ruined. Be especially careful when frying oysters—they can very quickly turn into hard, brown lumps.

Traditional Cape Cod Fried Oysters

SERVES 4

24 oysters, freshly shucked and drained
1/2 cup milk
1 egg, beaten
Tabasco to taste
1 cup cracker crumbs

Mix beaten egg and Tabasco with half a cup of milk. Dip the oysters in this mixture and roll them in cracker crumbs so they are well covered. Shake off the excess and fry the oysters in deep hot oil at 260 degrees for about 2½ to 3 minutes or until golden brown. Drain quickly on paper towels and serve at once.

NOTE: Chef Howard Mitcham suggests that the best results in frying oysters are had by using yellow corn flour (called Masa Harina in Latin American stores). He advises against using corn meal because it is too coarse and won't cook thoroughly in the short time required to cook an oyster. Clam fry mixes sold in New England stores are usually good because they are made of corn flour.

Fried Oysters Moutarde

SERVES 6
AS AN
APPETIZER

18 oysters, shucked
  (reserve and clean shells)
1 12-oz bottle of beer
1½ cups all-purpose flour
1 tablespoon paprika
1/2 teaspoon dry mustard
pinch of baking powder
pinch of salt
SAUCE:
2 cups heavy cream
1/2 cup dry white wine
1/4 cup Dijon mustard
1 small bay leaf
juice of 1/2 lemon
1 tablespoon fresh chopped parsley

In a glass bowl combine the beer, paprika, flour, baking powder, salt and mustard. Stir with a wire whisk until smooth. Coat each oyster in this batter and deep-fry at 350 degrees for approximately 1½ minutes or until the batter is crisp. Make sure the oysters are not overcooked. Drain and pat with paper towels.

Make the sauce by combining cream, mustard, wine, bay leaf, and lemon juice in a medium saucepan and simmer over moderate heat. Reduce mixture until about 1½ cups remain. Season with salt and pepper. To serve, spoon some sauce into each clean oyster shell and top with a fried oyster. Arrange on a platter and garnish with fresh chopped parsley.

Curried Corn & Oyster Chowder

SERVES 8

12 oysters, freshly shucked
2 oz butter
1/4 cup flour
1/4 cup sherry
curry power, soy sauce, and Tabasco to taste
1/2 teaspoon sugar
2 cans (16 oz) creamed corn
1 quart fish stock or chicken broth
1 cup heavy cream

Rinse oysters thoroughly and chop coarsely, reserving any liquor. Melt butter in a large, heavy pot. Mix in flour to form a roux. When flour is a light golden color, add sherry and seasonings, blending them in well. Mix in corn and stir to remove any lumps. Add the fish stock slowly, mixing soup well all the while. Pour in cream and heat, but do not boil. Add chopped oysters with their liquor and heat through but do not overcook. Serve immediately.

Oysters Gino

SERVES 4

24 oysters, freshly shucked (retain shells)

2 cups fresh crabmeat

juice of one lemon

couple of sprigs of fresh lemon thyme,
   finely chopped

pinch of white pepper

6 or 8 pieces of pancetta, cut into pieces
   (bacon may be substituted)

rock salt

BÉCHAMEL SAUCE:

4 tablespoons butter

4 tablespoons flour

2 cups milk, heated

pinch of nutmeg

freshly ground black pepper and salt to taste

To make the Béchamel Sauce, heat the butter in a saucepan over medium heat. Take the pan off the heat and stir in the flour to form a smooth paste. Return the pan to the to the heat and add the warmed milk, a little at a time, whisking thoroughly to incorporate it well. When all the milk has been added, turn heat to lowest setting and heat sauce gently for about 6 to 10 minutes. Add seasonings to taste and set aside.

Pick crabmeat over and remove any cartilage. Mix crabmeat into Béchamel sauce. Stir in the lemon juice, lemon thyme and white pepper.

Arrange the shucked oysters in their shells on rock salt in an oven-proof dish. Top each oyster with a spoonful of the crabmeat/bechamel mixture and a piece of pancetta. Bake at 375 degrees for 15 minutes or until the pancetta is crisp. Serve at once with lemon wedges.

Oysters Rockefeller

This delicious stuffing, distinctively flavored with Pernod or Anisette, also makes a wonderful dressing for baked or broiled fish.

<table>
<tr><td>SERVES 6</td><td>24 oysters
1/4 lb butter
1/2 package frozen chopped spinach
4 scallions, finely chopped
1 stalk celery, finely chopped
1 clove garlic, finely chopped
1/4 cup chopped parsley
1/4 cup white bread crumbs
1 teaspoon anchovy paste
2 teaspoons Worcestershire sauce
2 dashes Tabasco
1 tablespoon Pernod or Anisette
1/2 small head of lettuce, finely chopped,
   or 1/2 bunch watercress, finely chopped
half a lemon</td></tr>
</table>

Defrost spinach and press between paper towels to squeeze out the water. Chop vegetables and garlic finely by hand or in a food processor. Melt butter in a skillet and sauté the garlic and chopped vegetables until limp. Add the spinach and stir over medium heat for 2 minutes. Add the bread crumbs, anchovy paste, Worcestershire sauce, Tabasco, parsley, and seasonings, stirring in the Pernod last.

Open oysters and loosen from the shells. Place an oyster in the rounded half of each shell. Squeeze a couple of drops of lemon juice on each oyster and set them in rock salt in a baking pan. Cover each oyster with a spoonful of vegetable mixture and bake in a hot oven at 450 degrees for about 5 minutes. Serve at once, garnished with chopped lettuce or watercress.

Oysters Bienville

SERVES 2

12 oysters on the half shell (reserve liquor)
2 shallots, finely chopped
1 oz butter
1 tablespoon flour
1/2 cup chopped mushrooms
1/2 cup chopped shrimp
1 egg yolk
1/3 glass dry vermouth
dash of Tabasco

Sauté shallots in butter until translucent. Stir a tablespoon of flour into the butter and heat gently, stirring, until light golden brown. Stir in oyster liquor, shrimp, and mushrooms and mix well. Beat egg with vermouth in a separate bowl and add slowly to the sauce, beating rapidly. Season to taste. Simmer for 10 to 15 minutes, stirring constantly.

To serve, arrange oysters on rock salt on a platter and bake in the oven at 350 degrees until half done (about 6-7 minutes). Spoon sauce liberally over each oyster, sprinkle with paprika, and bake further until browned. Serve with lemon wedges.

You may like to top the oysters with a little grated cheese before baking.

Angels on Horseback

This gourmet version of a famed classic comes from the Impudent Oyster restaurant in Chatham.

SERVES 6 AS AN APPETIZER

30 oysters, shucked

15 strips of bacon, cut in half

6 slices country-style white bread

STUFFING:

1/2 cup fresh chopped parsley

1½ tablespoons finely minced onions

1 teaspoon fresh garlic, minced

SAUCE:

3 tablespoons freshly-squeezed lemon juice

1/2 cup heavy cream

1/2 lb unsalted chilled butter, cut into pieces

Mix the stuffing ingredients until well blended. Set aside. Pour lemon juice into a heavy saucepan and reduce to slightly less than half. Add the heavy cream and, over medium heat, reduce mixture to half, whisking frequently. Slowly add the chilled butter, one piece at a time, whisking all the while. Add a piece of butter when the previous one is half melted to maintain a consistent temperature. When the last piece has been added, remove immediately from heat and whisk until all the butter has melted completely. The sauce should get neither too hot nor too cold.

Place one oyster in the middle of each piece of bacon. Spoon about 1/2 teaspoon of stuffing over each oyster and roll up so that the stuffing is covered by the bacon. Secure with a toothpick. Place the oysters under a broiler for 3 or 4 minutes on each side, until bacon is cooked.

Toast bread and remove crusts. Cut toast pieces in half diagonally and place two toast points on each plate in a "stretched out" rectangle shape. Place five bacon-wrapped oysters, toothpicks removed, on each plate. Spoon sauce over oysters, and serve.

Celestial Oysters with Vermicelli

This main-course recipe is also a creation of the Impudent Oyster in Chatham

SERVES 6

36 oysters, freshly shucked
4 tablespoons butter
4 large shallots, diced
1 cup champagne
1/2 cup heavy cream
3 tablespoons roux
1½ cups Hollandaise sauce

Sauté the shallots quickly in hot butter over high heat. Add oysters and heat through. Pour in champagne and reduce quickly, being careful not to overcook the oysters. Remove oysters from pan with a slotted spoon and set aside.

Add cream and roux to pan juices and whisk thoroughly to make a smooth sauce. Return oysters to pan and heat through. Remove pan from heat and quickly whisk in warmed Hollandaise sauce. Serve on a bed of pasta, preferably vermicelli. Garnish with freshly-ground black pepper.

Pasta with Oysters & Scallops

12 shucked oysters and their liquor

10 sea scallops, cut into bite-sized pieces

1 tablespoon chopped leeks

2 teaspoons grated cheese

2 tablespoons white wine

2 cups white cream sauce

2 cups cooked spinach pasta

salt and pepper

1/4 cup chopped parsley

Heat a large pan of water to cook the pasta while you prepare the sauce.

Melt enough butter in a large sauté pan to cover the bottom. Add leeks and shellfish and simmer gently until cooked, about 3 to 5 minutes. Stir in the wine and cheese, and season with salt and pepper. Add the cream sauce and heat through.

Add cooked pasta to the pan and toss so pasta is well coated with the sauce. When the pasta is heated through, serve on heated plates and sprinkle with fresh chopped parsley.

Oyster Saffron Stew

SERVES 6

**18 oysters, shucked and cleaned
  (reserve liquor)**
3 tablespoons butter
**1 quart fish stock (clam juice may be
  substituted)**
1 large baking potato, peeled and diced
1 large carrot, chopped
1 large stalk celery, chopped
1 medium onion, chopped
1/2 lemon
**1 teaspoon dried saffron threads or
  powdered saffron**
**2 tablespoons chopped fresh dill, or
  1 teaspoon dried dill**
1/2 cup heavy cream
salt and white pepper to taste

Melt butter in a large saucepan. Add carrot, celery, and onion. Sauté over moderate heat for 10 minutes. Add fish stock, reserved oyster liquor, potato, lemon half, saffron, and fresh dill. Simmer for 20 minutes or until potatoes are tender. Let mixture cool a little and remove lemon half. Puree mixture in a blender or food processor. Reheat gently and add heavy cream and oysters. Simmer for a few minutes until the oysters are just cooked. The stew is ready when the oysters begin to curl. Be careful not to overcook the oysters. Season stew with salt and white pepper. Ladle into bowls and garnish with thinly sliced lemon and a sprig of fresh dill.

Classic Cape Cod Oyster Stew

SERVES 4

24 shucked oysters
2 tablespoons butter
1 medium onion, diced
1 large potato, cooked and diced
1 cup milk
1 cup light cream
2 cups oyster liquor (add water if necessary
  to make up quantity)
salt and white pepper to taste
paprika

Strain the oyster liquor to remove any grit and thoroughly wash the shucked oysters. Set aside.

Sauté the chopped onion lightly in butter until translucent, add the oysters and simmer for a few minutes. Add the oyster liquor and season with salt and pepper. Cook slowly for about 10 minutes. Add the diced potato and cook for a few minutes more. Stir in the milk and cream and heat through, being careful the milk does not boil. Serve piping hot in soup plates, garnished with a sprinkling of paprika.

Baked Oysters Claremont

SERVES 4

24 large oysters, shucked and drained

2 lbs fresh spinach

12 strips bacon

1/2 cup Parmesan cheese

OYSTER SAUCE:

2 cups mayonnaise

1/4 cup chili sauce

2 tablespoons Dijon mustard

1/2 teaspoon paprika

3-4 dashes Tabasco sauce

fresh lemon juice

salt and pepper to taste

Make the sauce by combining all ingredients, adding lemon, salt and pepper to individual taste.

Blanch spinach and squeeze well to remove as much moisture as possible. Chop spinach. Cook bacon until crisp and crumble bacon. Rinse the shucked oysters and place them in a shallow baking dish in a single layer and top with oyster sauce. Cover with spinach and bacon and top with a good sprinkling of Parmesan cheese. Bake at 375 degrees for 12 to 15 minutes or until cheese begins to brown.

Oyster Stuffing

FOR A 12 LB
TURKEY

18 oysters, freshly shucked and drained

24 slices dry bread, cubed

2/3 cup finely chopped turkey giblets

4 oz butter

2 cups finely chopped celery

1 cup finely chopped onion

1 teaspoon dried sage

1½ cups grated apple

2 cups water

1/2 teaspoon sugar

2 eggs, beaten

2½ teaspoons salt

1/4 teaspoon pepper

Cube or crumble the bread. Heat 2 oz of butter in a skillet and sauté the giblets for about 20 minutes over medium heat. Chop the oysters and vegetables and grate the apples. Heat 2 oz of butter in a large skillet and add the chopped celery, onion and apple. Cook over medium heat until the onion is translucent, stirring occasionally. Pour water over the bread, sprinkle on seasonings, and toss together gently. Add beaten eggs to seasoned bread and mix in well. Stir in oysters, giblets, vegetables, and apple and blend well together.

Rinse the turkey and pat dry with paper towels. Stuff the turkey, taking care not to pack in the stuffing too tightly. Any extra stuffing left over from the turkey may be cooked separately in a casserole for one hour in a medium oven.

Steak Stuffed with Oysters

SERVES 4

4 New York strip steaks, ³/₄" thick
1 tablespoon chopped garlic
4 oz softened butter
16 oysters, freshly shucked

With a sharp knife, cut a "pocket" running almost the entire length of each steak, making sure not to cut it completely in half. This should resemble the pocket shape of pita bread.

Blend the chopped garlic with softened butter. Stuff pockets with the butter mixture and then firmly pack each pocket with 4 oysters. Grill steaks to individual taste and serve sizzling hot.

Wellfleet Harbor in 1910.　　　　　　POSTCARD COURTESY NOEL W. BEYLE

Mitcham's Oysters en Brochette

"Many connoisseurs believe that this is absolutely the best way to cook and serve oysters. It requires a little skill and practice to get the method perfected."

—*from* CLAMS, MUSSELS, OYSTERS, SCALLOPS & SNAILS *by Howard Mitcham*

SERVES 4-6

36 oysters, shucked and drained
12 slices bacon
36 slices fresh mushrooms
corn flour
1/2 lb butter, melted
juice of 2 lemons
2 tablespoons chopped parsley
cayenne pepper

Fry the bacon over low heat in a skillet until almost done but still limp and not brown. Drain on paper towels. Cut each slice into three equal pieces and set aside. Melt the butter in a small saucepan, add the lemon juice and cayenne, and season with salt and black pepper. Mix well. Dip mushroom slices into the butter sauce to coat them. Dip oysters in the sauce to coat them, and sprinkle each oyster very lightly with corn flour.

Use 6 skewers. Fold a piece of bacon in half and spear with a skewer. Add an oyster, spearing it through the adductor muscles or "eye," and then add a slice of mushroom. Continue in this manner alternating bacon, oysters, and mushrooms until you have six of each on a skewer. Do not jam them closely together; leave spaces between them so the heat can get in there. There are several ways to cook them: grilled on a barbecue grill, broiled on a buttered cookie sheet under the broiler flame, or fried gently in butter in a large skillet. Turn them over once no matter how you're cooking them. Do not to overcook the oysters—cook them only until lightly browned and the bacon is crisp. Serve over toast on preheated serving plates. Heat what's left of the lemon-butter sauce in its saucepan and add the chopped parsley. Spoon equal amounts of this sauce on each serving. Serve at once, piping hot; don't let this get cold!

Pigs in Blankets

SERVES 2 AS AN APPETIZER	**12 shucked oysters** **6 slices bacon**

Cut the bacon slices in half. Fry the bacon slowly in a sauté pan until almost done but still limp. Wrap each bacon piece around an oyster and skewer with a cocktail toothpick. Arrange the wrapped oysters in a broiler pan and broil them on both sides until the bacon is brown and crispy, and the edges of the oysters curl. Serve at once hot in the pan.

Smoked Oysters

SERVES 4	**24 freshly-shucked oysters** **4 oz butter, softened** **2 cloves garlic, crushed**

Mix the butter with crushed garlic. Paint the oysters with garlic butter and wrap in tin foil. Smoke them over a hot charcoal fire for 5 minutes. Serve on a bed of lettuce, garnished with lemon wedges.

Falmouth Harbor

Scallops

Many consider the scallop the most delectable of our abundant local seafood, surpassing even the lobster for flavor, texture, and culinary versatility.

Scallops differ from clams, mussels, and other bivalve molluscs in that their shells never completely close. This means that whole scallops are especially prone to spoilage, and are therefore almost always shucked immediately after harvest, and virtually never sold in their shells. To further safeguard against spoilage, the scallop's gut is removed and discarded. What remains is the "eye" or adductor muscle, a sinew powerful enough to "jet" the scallop through the water by opening and closing its shell, creating hydraulic power. The scallop is the only bivalve mollusc that can actually jump and "swim"—scallops even migrate —and it's the only one with eyes, a row of bright blue primitive sight organs located on its mantle just inside the shell.

In Europe, the entire scallop is eaten, but in the States we only eat the adductor muscle and the rest is discarded, though occasionally the scallop is sold together with its reddish/orange roe or pale, creamy milt, both of which are delicious. Sometimes a tough filament remains attached to the side of the scallop; this should be cut off and discarded.

The two kinds of scallop found in Cape Cod waters are the bay, or Cape, scallop and the sea scallop. The bay scallop, which is more expensive and hard to come by, grows to about 2" wide and is the size of a small cork when shucked. They cook quickly and have a unique unusually sweet flavor. The season for bay scallops runs from early October until May. Calico scallops, from warmer waters off the Atlantic and Gulf coasts, can visually be confused with bay scallops, but for taste and texture there is no comparison—even though they are less than half the price of genuine bay scallops. Genuine aquacultured bay scallops, reared from a handful of scallops from Cape Cod, are now being imported from China; their price is somewhere between that of Cape scallops and calicos. These are real bay scallops and are quite good. The fast-growing Cape Cod aquaculture industry should be producing locally-grown bay scallops within a few years.

Sea scallops are harvested year-round in the waters off the Cape. Their shells can grow to eight or ten inches in diameter, and some, called "pie plates," get even bigger. The latter yields an adductor muscle that is the size of a small dinner roll. Scallops this large are cut into bite-sized pieces for most recipes.

The sweet, delicate flavor and fine texture of scallops render them a versatile ingredient for a great variety of recipes. The classic dish Coquilles St. Jacques is traditionally served in a large sea scallop shell, though small individual casserole dishes or pastry shells will do just as well. If you wish to use scallop shells for this purpose, ask a fisherman pal to bring you some. Boil them in a strong solution of water and bicarbonate of soda for an hour or more to clean and whiten them, but never use detergents or chemicals to clean the shells because they are porous and may transfer a strange taste to any food cooked in them. Coquilles St. Jacques—"Seashells of St. James"—are named after St. James, the patron saint of fishermen, whose symbol is the scallop shell. Pilgrims in the Middle Ages on their way to holy shrines dedicated to St. James wore scallop shells on their hats or around their necks. It was a crime to rob or molest a pilgrim who displayed this holy symbol.

Scallops need very little cooking—they should be heated just enough to render the translucent flesh opaque. Having said that, scallops are an integral ingredient in seviche, in which the cooking is done by acidity, not heat.

Smoked Scallops in Cream Sauce

This tasty appetizer comes from Mulligans Restaurant, at Ocean Edge in Brewster.

SERVES 6
AS AN
APPETIZER

3/4 lb smoked scallops

1 teaspoon minced shallots

1/2 teaspoon chopped garlic

1 teaspoon fresh chopped rosemary

2 tablespoons olive oil

1 cup heavy cream

1 tablespoon Pommery mustard

1 lb spinach

2 tablespoons butter

salt and pepper to taste

6 small pastry shells

Sauté shallots, garlic and rosemary in olive oil until the shallots are translucent. Stir in heavy cream and mustard and reduce until the sauce thickens. Warm the scallops in the cream sauce over low heat for a minute or two. Set aside.

Warm the pastry shells in a low oven for 10 minutes. Rinse the spinach and remove stems. Sauté spinach lightly in a skillet in 2 tablespoons of butter over medium heat. Season to taste with salt and pepper. Place a spoonful of wilted spinach in each pastry shell and top with smoked scallops in cream sauce, and serve.

Scallops Wrapped in Bacon

There's something heavenly about scallops and bacon cooked together. This recipe works well with oysters, too.

SERVES 4-6 AS
AN APPETIZER

Preheat oven to 400 degrees.

1 lb sea scallops, cut into 3/4" pieces

1 cup flour

1 tablespoon salt

1 tablespoon paprika

1 teaspoon ground pepper

1 teaspoon garlic powder

1 egg

1 cup milk

1 cup bread crumbs

1/2 lb bacon strips, cut into halves

Combine flour, salt, paprika, pepper, and garlic powder and place in a soup plate. Beat egg and milk together and place in a second soup plate. Place the bread crumbs in a third soup plate. Bread the scallops by dipping the scallops into the seasoned flour and shaking off any excess. Then dip into egg mixture, and then coat with bread crumbs, covering each scallop completely with crumbs. Wrap each scallop carefully in a half strip of bacon and secure with a toothpick. Place scallops in a baking pan and bake in oven until bacon is crisp, draining pan of liquid as necessary. Serve immediately.

Scotch & Scallop Bisque

This unusual recipe is from Donna Aliperti, chef/owner of Front Street Restaurant in Provincetown.

SERVES 4 - 6

1 lb scallops (slice or cube large sea scallops)

1 cup diced celery

1 cup diced onions

1/4 cup olive oil

4 tablespoons unsalted butter

1/2 cup flour

1/4 cup Scotch whisky

3 cups clam stock

1 cup half-and-half

1 teaspoon fresh thyme (or 1/2 teaspoon dried)

salt and pepper

Rinse scallops, pat dry and set aside. Heat the olive oil and butter in a heavy pot. Add onions and celery. Cook for 3 to 5 minutes or until onions are translucent. Dredge scallops in flour and add to the mixture Sauté over medium-high heat for 3 or 4 minutes. Stir in 2 tablespoons of flour and cook for another 3 minutes at medium heat. Add Scotch whisky and cook for one minute (if you are not used to flaming alcohol when cooking, remove pot from heat before adding the whisky, stir well, and return to heat). Pour in stock and half-and-half, and season with thyme. Add salt and pepper to taste and stir well. Let simmer on low heat for 10 minutes. Served garnished with a sprig of fresh thyme or parsley and a dash of paprika.

For a unique taste, you may substitute Triple Sec for the whisky to create a Mandarin scallop bisque.

Scallop Bisque with Caviar

This recipe is also delightful served chilled, garnished with fresh chopped coriander and a slice of lime.

SERVES 4

1 lb scallops, rinsed and trimmed (make sure the tough muscle filament on side is removed)

1 shallot, finely minced

3 tablespoons unsalted butter

3 tablespoons flour

2 cups chicken stock

2 cups fish stock

1/2 cup dry white wine

2 egg yolks

1/2 cup heavy cream

pinch cayenne pepper

American Golden Caviar or lumpfish caviar to garnish

Sauté shallots in butter until they are translucent. Add flour and stir over low heat for 8 minutes. Be careful not to let the roux brown. Combine chicken and fish stocks in a saucepan and bring to a boil, removing scum if necessary. Add half a cup of white wine. Add this stock to the roux gradually, whisking the mixture over a low flame. Season with cayenne pepper, strain, and return to the saucepan.

Puree scallops in a food processor and add to the soup. Whisk heavy cream and egg yolks together in a bowl and slowly pour 2 ladles of the soup onto the egg and cream mixture, whisking well as it is added. Return this mixture to the soup and heat through. Thin with light cream if necessary. Garnish with caviar just before serving.

Scallops Addington

I was given this tasty recipe by Ray Keyton, former owner of the Café at the Mews in Provincetown, quite a few years back, when Molly O'Neill was the chef there.

SERVES 4

2 lbs bay or sea scallops

2 tablespoons olive oil or butter

1/2 teaspoon finely chopped garlic

6 artichoke hearts, cut into halves

1 cup heavy cream

1/4 cup dry vermouth

1/2 cup grated Asiago cheese (fresh grated
   Parmesan cheese may be substituted)

pinch of black pepper

Rinse scallops and pat dry with paper towels. Cut large sea scallops into smaller pieces. In a large pan, lightly sauté the scallops in butter or oil. Add garlic and continue to sauté until garlic releases its flavor. Add halved artichokes. Pour in the vermouth and deglaze the pan. Stir in the heavy cream and black pepper and reduce over high heat for one or two minutes. Stir in the grated cheese until it melts. Portion the mixture into 4 individual ovenproof dishes and place under the broiler for a few minutes until the tops are lightly brown. Serve immediately.

Baked Scallops with Crabmeat Stuffing

SERVES 4

1 lb sea scallops, cut into bite-sized pieces

7 oz crab meat

4 cups fine white bread crumbs

1 onion, minced

2 cloves garlic, minced

4 oz butter

1/4 teaspoon salt

1/4 teaspoon white pepper

dash of thyme

1/4 cup chopped parsley

1/2 wine glass sherry, or to taste

1/4 cup olive oil

Sauté minced onions and garlic in butter. In a large bowl mix bread crumbs, crab meat, salt, pepper, thyme, and chopped parsley. Mix oil and sherry alternately in small amounts until the stuffing is moist. Place a layer of scallops in a buttered baking dish with a layer of stuffing on top. Continued layering scallops and stuffing, ending with a layer of stuffing. Top with a little butter and bake in a medium oven for 20 minutes, or until browned on top.

Scallops & Mussels Royale

SERVES 1

4 oz scallops

10 mussels

1 oz unsalted butter

1 oz fresh mushrooms, sliced

1 clove shallots, minced

1/2 oz malt whisky

juice of 1/2 lemon

1 oz heavy cream

pinch of fresh chopped parsley

Rinse scallops, halve or quarter large ones, and set aside. Scrub and debeard mussels. Steam in a covered pot for a few minutes until shells open. Reserve mussels and discard shells.

Place butter, mushrooms, scallops, and shallots in a sauté pan and slowly cook for 2 to 3 minutes. Add the whisky and flame. When flame has subsided, stir in cream, parsley, lemon juice, and add the mussels. Cook slowly until cream thickens, and serve with rice or pasta.

Scallops Pernod

The Pernod lends a lovely flavor to this dish, one of my favorites at Napi's Restaurant in Provincetown.

SERVES 2 | **1 lb scallops, cut into bite-sized pieces**
pinch of chopped fresh tarragon
4 tablespoons butter
1/2 teaspoon Pernod
1/2 cup heavy cream

Sauté the scallops quickly in butter with a pinch of tarragon. When lightly golden, add about half a teaspoon of Pernod—you need only a hint of it. Add the cream to the pan and stir, letting the scallops and cream cook for about 3 minutes until the flavors blend and the sauce thickens. Serve with rice or pasta.

Seining fish in Provincetown Harbor, 1906.   POSTCARD COURTESY OF NOEL W. BEYLE

Scallops Framboise

This delicately flavored dish, where the tartness of raspberries offsets the richness of the scallops, is served at Aesop's Tables in Wellfleet.

SERVES 2

1 lb bay scallops

1/2 cup white wine

1 teaspoon minced shallots

1 teaspoon sugar

1 teaspoon fresh chopped thyme

1/2 cup fresh raspberries

1/3 cup butter

juice from one lemon

Marinate the raspberries and thyme in the white wine, shallots, and sugar for 45 minutes to an hour. Then simmer this mixture over medium heat for 10–15 minutes, reducing it to a sticky, translucent liquid. Strain the liquid and return to the pan. Add butter to the strained liquid and melt over low heat, stirring well to make a sauce. Broil the scallops for two minutes in lemon juice and a little water. Pour a puddle of the sauce on each serving plate and place the broiled scallops on top of the sauce. Garnish with fresh raspberries.

Coquilles St. Jacques with Mushrooms

From "Clams, Mussels, Oysters, Scallops and Snails" *by Howard Mitcham, Provincetown's seafood chef extraordinaire.*

Serves 4 - 6

1 lb sea scallops, cut in quarters

12 oz small mushrooms

1 cup half-and-half

4 oz butter

3 tablespoons flour

1/2 cup dry sherry

1/2 teaspoon salt

freshly ground black pepper to taste

dash of Tabasco

paprika

Wipe off the tops of the mushrooms with a damp cloth (never wash fresh mushrooms, the water makes their gills soggy and difficult to cook properly.) Slice the mushrooms, melt 2 oz of butter in a skillet and sauté the mushrooms until they are cooked but not browned. Place in a bowl and set aside in a warm place.

Melt the other 2 oz of butter in the skillet, add flour and cook over a low fire, stirring until well blended. Add the half-and-half and cook, stirring, until the sauce thickens. Add the scallops, sherry, mushrooms, Tabasco, salt and freshly ground black pepper. Mix well and cook for 10 minutes longer, or until the scallops are opaque and white. Serve in heated scallop shells, or warm pastry shells, or in individual casseroles. Sprinkle the top with a dash of paprika and serve at once.

Coquilles St. Jacques à l'Orientale

This inspired dish, rich and delicious, comes from Astrid Berg, chef at Pepe's Wharf in Provincetown. It is especially delectable served in a puff pastry shell as a main course.

SERVES 4 AS AN APPETIZER, 2 AS A MAIN COURSE

Preheat oven to 475 degrees

16 sea scallops

1/4 lb shiitake mushrooms

1 shallot, minced

1/3 cup dry white wine

2 teaspoons white wine vinegar

10 tablespoons unsalted butter, softened slightly

1½ tablespoons lemon juice

1/2 teaspoon soy sauce

pinch of curry powder

salt and freshly ground pepper

1 tablespoon olive oil

coarse sea salt

Rinse and dry mushrooms and slice thinly. In a small saucepan combine shallots, wine, vinegar, and 1 tablespoon of water. Bring to a boil and cook until almost all the liquid has evaporated (about 2 minutes). Reduce heat to low and whisk in butter, 2 tablespoons at a time. Add lemon juice, soy sauce, and curry powder, and season to taste with salt and pepper. Strain sauce and keep warm over hot water. Place scallops on a lightly buttered baking sheet and bake without turning just until scallops whiten and lose their opaque quality (about 6-8 minutes). Heat olive oil in a skillet and sauté mushrooms over high heat until lightly browned. Drain on paper towels.

To serve, ladle a generous spoonful of sauce onto each plate and spoon scallops on top, brown side up. Sprinkle with sea salt and freshly ground black pepper and top with browned mushrooms.

Coquilles Venetian

Here is another delicious scallop recipe I was given by Ray Keyton of the Café at the Mews in Provincetown some years back.

SERVES 4

2 lbs bay or sea scallops
flour for dredging
butter or olive oil
1 lb spinach, washed well and chopped
1 cup peeled, chopped and deseeded cucumber
2 tablespoons chopped tarragon,
  fresh if possible
splash of raspberry vinegar
salt and pepper to taste
1/2 cup heavy cream
lemon wedges for garnish

Rinse the scallops, pat dry, and dredge in flour. Shake vigorously to remove excess flour. Sauté the scallops lightly in butter or oil and drain off fat. Mix together the spinach, cucumber, tarragon, and raspberry vinegar. Add the spinach mixture to the pan and sauté for one minute, stirring briskly. Season to taste with salt and pepper. Stir in the heavy cream and reduce for one or two minutes to make a sauce. Serve immediately garnished with lemon wedges.

Cape Scallops Darla

As served by the late Howard Gruber, cofounder and chef of Front Street Restaurant in Provincetown.

SERVES 2

1¹/₂ lbs bay scallops, or sea scallops
    cut into quarters
1/2 lb mushrooms
3 tablespoons capers, salted or in brine
4 tablespoons butter
5 shallots, peeled and minced
6 artichoke hearts, quartered
1/4 cup of a mixture of sweet and dry vermouth
juice of 1/2 lemon
1/4 cup heavy cream
chopped parsley

Wipe mushrooms clean and slice thinly. Wash the capers thoroughly. Remove the tough muscles from the sides of the scallops and dust them in flour seasoned with salt and pepper.

Heat the butter in a sauté pan and add the shallots. Sauté for a few minutes. Add the mushroom slices and capers and cook until mushrooms are semisoft, about 3 minutes. Remove from the pan with a slotted spoon and add the floured scallops. Brown the scallops quickly, adding more butter if necessary. Return the mushroom mixture to the pan with the artichoke hearts. Stir the ingredients around a bit and scrape the bottom of the pan. Add the vermouth and lemon juice (you may put the squeezed lemon in the pan for extra flavor), and cover for one minute to let the vermouth cook off. Stir in the heavy cream and cook for one more minute. This should all happen quickly—take care not to overcook the scallops. Spoon onto a serving platter and serve garnished with chopped parsley and lemon wedges.

Scallop Casserole

The next two recipes come from Mary Alice Luiz Cook's
TRADITIONAL PORTUGUESE RECIPES FROM PROVINCETOWN.

SERVES 4

*Preheat
oven to
350 degrees.*

1 lb bay scallops, or sea scallops, cut into bite-sized pieces

1 cup cracker meal or crumbs

milk to cover

paprika

salt and pepper to taste

4 oz butter

2 oz grated cheese

Place the scallops and crumbs in layers in a casserole dish and pour enough milk over the scallops to cover them. Add seasonings. Scatter a few thick slices of butter on top. Sprinkle with more crumbs, and top with more pieces of butter. Sprinkle with paprika.

Bake in the oven at 350 degrees for about 25 minutes. Sprinkle with grated cheese about 10 minutes before it has finished cooking. Let sit for 10 minutes or so before serving.

Scallop Stew

SERVES 2

1 pint bay scallops, or sea scallops, quartered
1 onion, sliced thinly
4 oz butter
1 quart milk
1 large potato, cooked and diced
salt and pepper to taste
paprika

Fry out onion slices lightly in butter, being careful not to brown them. Add scallops and stir the into the butter slowly. Simmer for a few minutes and set aside. Add the cooked diced potatoes to the scallops, then slowly add the milk. Simmer gently for about 10 minutes, but be careful not to let the stew come to a boil. Season to taste. To serve, spoon into individual soup plates and sprinkle with paprika.

Boat landing at Barnstable Harbor, c. 1920.   POSTCARD COURTESY OF NOEL W. BEYLE

Scallop & Crabmeat Casserole

This scallop casserole, from the village of Peniche in Portugal, is served at the Moors Restaurant in Provincetown with the title: "Carangueijo Vieira a Moda de Peniche."

SERVES 4

Lobster meat may be substituted for crab-meat.

12 oz fresh scallops, cut into bite-sized pieces

12 oz king crabmeat

2 teaspoons butter

1/4 cup each dry white port and brandy

THE SAUCE:

2 medium-sized onions, minced

3 tablespoons butter

6 tomatoes, peeled, seeded and chopped

2 large cloves garlic, minced or sliced

1 bay leaf

1/3 cup chopped fresh parsley

1 1/2 teaspoons ground mustard

1/2 teaspoon paprika

1/4 teaspoon ground nutmeg

1/8 teaspoon crushed dried hot red peppers

1/8 teaspoon sugar

1/2 cup white table wine

In a frying pan, sauté onions in three tablespoons of butter until limp. Add tomatoes, garlic, bay leaf, parsley, mustard, paprika, nutmeg, hot peppers, sugar, and dry white wine. Season to taste with salt and pepper. Simmer, loosely covered, for 30 minutes or until reduced to a very thick sauce. Stir occasionally. Remove from heat and stir in two teaspoons of butter with the port and the brandy. Arrange half the crabmeat and half the scallops in a layer over the bottom of a top-of-the-stove casserole (2 to 2 1/2 quarts), and cover with half the sauce. Top with the remaining crabmeat, scallops, and sauce. Cover and simmer for 15 minutes or until the scallops are cooked through. Serve with rice as an accompaniment.

Seviche

This recipe was given to me by Dan de Palma, former owner of the Landmark Restaurant in Provincetown, with this tale about its origins: "We were introduced to this appetizer on our first trip to Mexico City many years ago when we dined at a private home where this seviche was served by our hostess. The idea of eating uncooked fish had little appeal to us then, but it was presented in a lettuce cup and garnished with a large hibiscus blossom and proved as tantalizing to our palates as it was to the eye—and our hostess was delighted to share her recipe with us."

SERVES 6

1 lb whole bay scallops, no larger than your
    baby finger nail, or sea scallops, quartered
1/2 lb sole fillets
1/2 lb haddock fillets
1 large Bermuda onion, sliced paper thin
1 large sweet pepper, sliced paper thin
juice of 12 freshly-squeezed limes
juice of 3 freshly-squeezed lemons
1/2 cup chopped ripe or green pitted olives
1 tablespoon coarsely ground black pepper
2 tablespoons capers
1 cup finely diced celery
1 2-oz jar chopped pimientos, drained
pinch of curry powder and paprika

With a sharp knife, cut the fish into very thin slices and place with the scallops in a large ceramic or glass bowl. DO NOT USE A PLASTIC, WOODEN, OR METAL BOWL. Add all the other ingredients—except the curry powder and paprika—and gently mix together. Cover and refrigerate for at least 24 hours. Turn the ingredients about every 6 hours to be sure everything is well coated with marinade; this is what "cooks" the seafood. To serve, portion equal amounts of seviche onto a bed of lettuce leaves on each serving plate and sprinkle with a pinch of powdered curry powder and paprika. Seviche is best served within three days after being marinated for at least 24 hours.

Lobster boats moored in Chatham Harbor.

Lobster

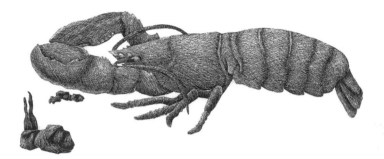

The lobster—now recognized internationally as a symbol of gourmet fare—had a humble start. Back in the 1600s, the first settlers used these then-plentiful crustaccans as fertilizer for their crops, but they soon discovered they were good enough to eat, for early records show that Cape Codders were selling their lobsters in Boston for three half-pence each in 1740.

The lobster fishing industry really took off after 1800 and in 1812, the people of Provincetown had a law passed through the State Legislature barring out-of-state fishermen from sharing their bounty, for stories tell of lobsters so thick on the beach at low tide that fishermen could go out and fill wheelbarrows with them. These same fishermen, legend has it, sailed up to Maine to show the locals there how to manage their own lobster fisheries, probably in an attempt to safeguard their own bountiful supply.

Lobsters grow slowly—it takes five years for a lobster to reach a pound in size and as many as 20 years to reach four pounds. There are reports of giant lobsters as long as six feet being caught in the past, but the area has been heavily fished for many years, and now the sizes most often found in local waters are "chickens" (one-pounders), or "quarters" (one-and-a-quarter-pounders). A chicken lobster yields about four ounces of meat. You can usually come across two, three, and four-pounders, and occasionally one as large as 15 pounds, sometimes kept as a mascot in a fish market tank. Happily for lobster lovers, this favorite of all seafood is unlikely to become scarce because lobsters are migratory and those caught along the eastern coast of Cape Cod are only the fringe of a much larger migratory group, rather than representative of a local colony.

Most lobsters are harvested from late spring through late fall when they migrate closer to the shore. They populate the sandy bottom of the ocean searching for food and are caught in lobster traps, sometimes in fishing nets, or by scuba divers who pick them right off the ocean floor. Lobsters molt or shed their shells about once a year, usually during the summer. These soft-shell lobsters, or "shedders," have a smaller meat-to-shell ratio than hard-shells because they hibernate and do not eat while in this phase. They also tend to fill with water as they are cooked. Some people believe that shedders have sweeter meat, but most prefer hard-shelled lobsters. Others swear that smaller lobsters are sweeter than larger ones—myself included—but this is one of those seafood discussions that never ends.

Cooking lobsters properly is of paramount importance. Steamed is best, but for *exactly* the right amount of time: 15 minutes for a one-pounder, five minutes more for each additional pound. And the fresher the better—a lobster should be alive and kicking. If it's "sleepy," it means that its flavor has already begun to deteriorate. Though lobsters have no "nerves" or pain receptors and only possess a quite primitive pre-brain, some cooks prefer to kill a lobster before cooking it by plunging a sharp knife point into the cross-mark on the lobster's head. This kills it instantly. This technique is also handy for lobsters before they are split for grilling or cut up for stir-frying.

People who've only seen a cooked lobster may not realize that live lobsters are a dark bluish-green color. They turn a bright red when cooked, and a little vinegar in the boiling water increases the intensity of the red.

Boiled Lobster

This is Mary Alice Luiz Cook's method for cooking and eating lobster from her book, TRADITIONAL PORTUGUESE RECIPES FROM PROVINCETOWN.

SERVES 4

1^1/$_4$ lb lobster per person
1 lb butter, clarified
1 tablespoon vinegar
2 lemons, cut into quarters

Place enough water in a large pot to half cover the lobsters. (Clean seawater adds subtly to the flavor, as does adding a handful of fresh seaweed to the water.) Add a tablespoon of vinegar—this helps the flavor and makes the shells a brilliant red when cooked. When the water has boiled, place the lobsters in the water head first (putting lobsters in the refrigerator before cooking will chill them and they will feel nothing.) Cover the pot and bring to the boil again. Timing from this point, boil until the lobsters turn bright red and one of the small feelers breaks off easily (about 12 to 15 minutes, depending on size—do not overcook or the lobsters will be tough.) If you are not sure the lobster is cooked, break the tail halfway off and if the tail meat is transparent and soft, it needs more steaming; if the meat is opaque and firm, then it is done. Remove the lobsters from the pot and place on a platter. Let them sit for about 5 minutes so the water can drain off before serving. You may want to poke a hole in the cross-mark on top of the lobster's head and drain some of the water out.

To clarify butter: Heat a pound of butter in a small pan. Skim off the foam and let it sit in the pan until all the water, salt, and other bits sink to the bottom. Pour off the clarified butter, leaving the white residue in the bottom of the pan.

To eat a lobster: Break off the large claws and crack them with a hammer or nutcracker. Pull or push out the meat with a small lobster fork or pick. Break the head off from the tail by grasping the head in one hand and the tail in the other and bending or twisting the head off.

Break the flippers off the end of the tail and push the tail meat out of the shell from the flipper end with a pick or small fork. In the head you will find the roe, or coral, and tomalley—some people think this is the best part of the lobster, try it before you throw it out. If you are patient, you will find plenty of lobster meat in the head.

Dip each morsel in warm clarified butter and sprinkle with fresh lemon juice. Delicious!

Grilled Lobster

Lobsters may be grilled whole, but as they tend to get dry and the claws have a tendency to become overcooked by the time the tail meat is done, it is best to split them first. They will then grill evenly and quickly.

Kill lobsters first by plunging a sharp knife point into the cross mark on the head. Cut them in half lengthwise with a cleaver and remove the stomach and intestine. The tomalley (which is a gray/green paste) and roe (an orange/yellow mass, found occasionally in females) can remain. Grill the lobster over a charcoal fire for about 5 minutes on its back to firm up the meat. Turn it over, sprinkle with salt and pepper, and grill for another 8 minutes or so on the other side. Lobster meat is cooked when it is firm and white. Serve with lemon quarters and clarified or melted butter. You may also like to paint the lobster meat with garlic butter before grilling for a special gourmet treat.

Lobster Chowder

SERVES 8

4 lobster backs
1/2 lb cooked lobster meat
2½ cups chopped onions
2 bay leaves
2 celery ribs, chopped
pinch of salt
3 large potatoes, peeled and diced
WHITE SAUCE:
1/4 lb butter
3/4 cup flour
1 cup milk
1 cup light cream, more if needed
pinch of salt, pepper and nutmeg

Heat 3 cups of water in a stock pot and simmer the celery, bay leaves, and lobster backs with one cup of chopped onions. Add a pinch of salt and cook for 30 minutes. Remove the lobster backs and set aside. Strain the stock. Scrape any tomalley and scraps of lobster meat from the lobster backs and add to the stock. Add diced potatoes and the remaining chopped onions and cook gently until the vegetables are tender, about 20 minutes. Remove chowder from the heat and set aside.

To make the white sauce, melt the butter in a saucepan and stir in the flour. Cook, stirring, so the flour cooks but does not brown. Warm the milk and stir gradually into the roux until the mixture thickens. Stir in the cream and season to taste. Add to the chowder and stir until it thickens, but do not boil. Add more cream or milk if the chowder seems too thick for your taste. Check seasonings and reheat gently before serving.

Lobster Bisque

SERVES 4

4 to 8 lobster bodies, cooked
1/4 cup butter
1 medium-sized onion, peeled and chopped
1 clove garlic, peeled and chopped
1 medium-sized carrot, chopped
1 bay leaf
1/2 teaspoon dried thyme, or 1 teaspoon fresh
1 cup dry white wine
1 cup chopped tomatoes
6 cups fish or chicken stock, or strained liquid
**   reserved from boiling lobsters**
1 cup heavy cream
salt and freshly-ground black pepper to taste

Sauté the onions, garlic, carrot, bay leaf, and thyme in butter over medium heat until the onion softens. Add the lobster bodies, and also any lobster shells you can find, along with any tomalley and coral. Cook, stirring, for about 5 minutes. Add the wine and chopped tomatoes and bring to a gentle boil. Lower the heat and simmer, covered, for 10 minutes. Add the stock, bring mixture to a boil, and return to a simmer for another 2 minutes. Remove the bay leaf and the lobster shells, scraping off any meat and returning it to the bisque.

Blend the bisque in a blender or food processor until smooth. Return soup to the pot and bring to a boil. Add the remaining butter in bits until it melts. Add the cream and any lobster meat you have scraped from the shells, and heat through. Check for seasoning and serve, garnished with chopped parsley.

Lobster Quiche

SERVES 4-6

1/2 cup cooked lobster meat
1/4 cup diced onions
6 large mushrooms, sliced
1 tablespoon olive oil
1/4 cup white wine
pinch of thyme
1/3 pint light cream or half-and-half
4 eggs
pinch of nutmeg
salt and freshly-ground black pepper to taste
1 precooked pie crust

Sauté onions and mushrooms in the oil and white wine. Season with a pinch of thyme. When the vegetables are soft, drain and set aside.

Lay the cooked lobster meat on the bottom of the pie crust and top with onions and mushrooms. Beat the cream with the eggs and season with salt, pepper, and a pinch of nutmeg. Pour this batter over the lobster meat and sautéed vegetables. Place the quiche carefully in a preheated oven and cook for 10 minutes at 450 degrees. Reduce the heat to 350 degrees and cook for 35 or 40 minutes more or until the quiche has risen and the top is golden brown. When cooked, the quiche will remain firm when shaken. Let it stand for 10 minutes or so before serving.

Lobster Kendall

This creamy lobster casserole, with just a hint of sweetness, was created by the late Kendall Bowers, who founded the delightful Arbor Restaurant in Orleans in 1972.

SERVES 2

Preheat oven to 450 degrees.

8 oz lobster meat, cut into bite-sized chunks

8 oz scallops, halved or quartered

2 tablespoons chopped leeks

1/2 cup sliced mushrooms

1/8 cup dark raisins

1 oz butter

2 tablespoons port wine

2 cups light cream sauce

salt and pepper to taste

Lightly sauté the lobster meat, scallops, leeks, mushrooms, and raisins in butter until cooked, about 5 minutes. Add the port wine, salt, and pepper and heat through. Stir in the cream sauce and simmer for about 5 minutes. Serve in individual casserole dishes garnished with chopped parsley.

Fettucine with Lobster

*This simple but delectable dish comes from Ciro Cozzi of Ciro & Sal's,
Provincetown's popular Italian restaurant.*

SERVES 1

1 lobster tail
1 oz butter
pinch of chopped tarragon
1/2 wine glass white wine
1 cup heavy cream
salt and pepper to taste
basil leaves for garnish
1/3 lb fettucine

Sauté the lobster tail gently in butter, tarragon, and white wine. Take care
not to overcook. When opaque, slice the lobster tail in the pan and add
the cream. Season to taste with salt and pepper and stir until the cream
is warmed through and the flavors have blended. Cook the pasta al
dente. Serve the sauce over fettucine and garnish with fresh basil leaves.

Chilled Poached Lobster with Caviar Mayonnaise

This summertime favorite comes from Sweet Seasons Restaurant at the Inn at Duck Creeke in Wellfleet.

SERVES 4

4 1½-lb lobsters

2 bay leaves

1 teaspoon peppercorns

1/2 cup white wine or clam juice

CAVIAR MAYONNAISE:

2 eggs

3 tablespoons vinegar

2/3 teaspoon salt

1/2 teaspoon white pepper

2 teaspoons Dijon mustard

2 cups olive oil

2-4 tablespoons lemon juice

2 tablespoons boiling water

1 small jar red caviar

GARNISH:

black olives

fresh parsley

lemon wedges

sliced hard-boiled eggs

To make the mayonnaise, place all ingredients—except 1½ cups of olive oil, the lemon juice and water—in a blender. Blend at medium speed. Continue to blend this mixture while adding the rest of the oil in a slow thin stream. When all the oil has been blended in, add lemon juice to taste and blend in once again. Check seasoning and blend in 2 tablespoons of hot water. Chill for at least 2 hours. Carefully fold in 3 tea-spoons of red caviar before serving.

Place one inch of water and half a cup of white wine or clam juice in a large pot with a tight-fitting lid. Add the bay leaves and peppercorns. Cover the pot and bring the liquid to a slow simmer. Place the lobsters into the pot and cover. Cook for 15 minutes. Remove lobsters and refrigerate until chilled.

To serve, remove the claws from the lobsters and crack with a cleaver. Twist the lobster tails from the bodies. Cut each tail lengthwise in the shell with kitchen shears or a sharp knife Remove the long black intestinal thread. Remove the sac from between the eyes and discard. Save the tomalley and roe—they are delicious mixed with a little of the mayonnaise, served on crackers or toast. Pick any meat from inside the body cavities and stir into the mayonnaise.

Place lettuce leaves in the four body cavities and fill with caviar mayonnaise. Cover a serving platter with lettuce leaves and arrange the lobster tails and claws around the four lobster bodies. Garnish with black olives, parsley, wedges of lemon, and sliced hard-boiled eggs.

Lobster Wonton Dumplings

If you are lucky, you might find these on the menu at The Mews waterfront restaurant in Provincetown when you next go there for dinner.

SERVES 4

1 cup cooked lobster meat cut into small chunks

20 round wonton wrappers

1 tablespoon peanut oil

1 teaspoon heavy sesame oil

2 teaspoons minced peeled ginger

2 teaspoons minced garlic

4 tablespoons oyster sauce

1 teaspoon Chinese chili sauce

4 tablespoons dry sherry

3 scallions, chopped

2 tablespoons cornstarch mixed with
    2 tablespoons cold water

Heat the peanut and sesame oils in a medium-sized sauté pan. When hot, sauté ginger and garlic, taking care not to brown the garlic. Toss in the oyster sauce, chili sauce, and sherry mix and continue to sauté. Add the lobster meat and scallions. When the mixture starts to bubble, thicken with half of the cornstarch/water mixture. The final mixture should be of a porridge consistency. This is a quick process and takes less than a minute. Remove mixture from the stove and let cool for half an hour.

Brush the wonton wrappers with the remaining cornstarch mixture. With a teaspoon, drop a little of the lobster filling into the center of each wonton. Fold the wonton wrapper in half, making sure that the edges are sealed and any air that might be trapped in the lobster filling has been worked out of the wrappers. Now place the stuffed wrapper in the palm of your hand, straight side facing your fingers. Moisten the edge closest to your thumb and bring the other edge over to seal it on top of the moistened edge. The wonton dumplings should look like a wide-brimmed hat. Repeat with all the remaining wrappers.

When all the wonton dumplings have been formed, drop them into a large pot of boiling water and cook until dumplings rise to the surface of the water, about 3 minutes. Remove, drain and serve with your favorite dipping sauces.

Lobster Enchiladas

SERVES 4

8 oz cooked lobster meat

1½ cups grated Monterey Jack cheese

1/2 cup grated Cheddar cheese

4 corn tortillas

1 cup enchilada or ranchero sauce

Soften tortillas by dipping them briefly into hot oil, one at a time, giving them only a few seconds to soften. Drain briefly on paper towels.

Spread all four tortillas out on a counter top or cutting board. Fill with lobster meat and grated cheeses. Roll up the enchiladas and place seam-side down in a baking dish. Cover with a thin coating of sauce and top with a little grated cheese. Bake in an oven for 20 minutes at 350 degrees. Serve hot with fresh salsa on the side.

Lobster Newburg

Howard Mitcham, the "Cape Tip Gourmet," perfected this recipe for Lobster Newburg for publication in his book THE PROVINCETOWN SEAFOOD COOKBOOK.

SERVES 2

2 cups lobster meat, cut into chunks

1 oz butter

2 tablespoons brandy

2 cups Newburg sauce

NEWBURG SAUCE:

1 oz butter

3 tablespoons flour

1 cup cream

1 cup milk

1 cup evaporated milk

3/4 teaspoon salt

1/4 teaspoon freshly-ground black pepper

pinch ground nutmeg

1/4 cup sherry

1/4 cup chopped mushrooms

To make Newburg sauce, melt the butter in a saucepan, remove from the heat, and stir in the flour. Mix it well with the butter. Add the cream a little at a time at first, stirring constantly. Then add the milk and evaporated milk. Return to the heat and cook slowly, stirring all the time. Add the salt, pepper, nutmeg, sherry, and mushrooms. Keep cooking, stirring constantly, until the sauce thickens. If necessary, add more milk if the sauce seems to thick.

Don't try to cook more than two helpings of lobster Newburg at a time; it fouls things up.

Melt 1 oz of butter in a skillet and add the lobster meat and brandy. Flame the brandy. Sauté gently until the lobster is lightly cooked. Add 2 cups of Newburg sauce and cook for 3 or 4 minutes longer, stirring carefully so as not to break up the lobster chunks. Makes two generous helpings.

Serve it in individual casserole dishes with toast triangles and rice on the side. A good light white wine will counteract the richness of this dish.

"I've wrestled for years with various classic Newburg recipes, twisting them around to find one that I really felt proud of. I eliminated eggs from the formula; with good butter, cream, brandy, and sherry, the sauce is rich enough. Omitting the eggs simplifies the cooking process also. And there's the evaporated milk that I've added–everybody who ever ate a chowder knows that one-half milk plus one-half evaporated milk gives a much better chowder than plain milk does, and it does something for Newburg sauce, too. And I've thrown in a few chopped fresh mushrooms just for the hell of it. The purists will howl but that's my formula which has pleased many gourmets."   — HOWARD MITCHAM

Lobster Thermidor

SERVES 2

1 1¼ lb lobster

1 teaspoon chopped shallots or green onions

2 tablespoons butter

1/3 lb mushrooms, quartered

4 artichoke hearts, quartered

2 tablespoons flour

1 teaspoon dry mustard

1 tablespoon brandy

2/3 cup white wine

1/2 cup heavy cream

Steam lobster in a pot with a tight-fitting lid for about 5 minutes. Remove from pot and allow to cool slightly. When cool, split the lobster down its entire length so it is cut in 2 pieces. Clean the chest cavity completely and rinse out. Remove tail meat and claw meat and cut into bite-sized chunks.

Sauté shallots in butter until soft. Add mushrooms, artichoke quarters and lobster meat and cook until mushrooms are almost cooked through. Add flour and mustard and cook for a minute, stirring constantly. Add brandy and wine and simmer for about 2 minutes. Add heavy cream and bring back to almost a boil, stirring continuously.

To serve, arrange the empty shell of each half lobster on a plate and spoon the lobster mixture back into the shell. Garnish with lemon wedges and parsley.

Chicken Homard

This delicious and impressive-looking dish comes from the
Roadhouse Café in Hyannis.

SERVES 4

Preheat
oven to
400
degrees.

4 chicken breasts, 8 oz each

6 oz fresh lobster meat, cooked

8 slices Swiss cheese (about 1/2 lb)

flour, egg wash, and bread crumbs for dredging

CREAM SAUCE:

1/4 lb butter

1/4 cup white wine

pinch of lemon pepper

3 fresh lemons, squeezed

2 tablespoons roux

pinch of chopped fresh garlic

1/2 cup heavy cream

1/4 cup Parmesan cheese

3 tablespoons fresh chopped parsley

Pound each chicken breast flat until it is about 1½ times its original size. Place two slices of Swiss cheese on the bottom inside portion of each chicken breast. Place 1/4 of the lobster meat on the cheese. Roll up the Swiss cheese, catching the bottom of the chicken breast as you go. As you roll, fold in the sides of the chicken to make a round package. Press the edges firmly so the stuffed chicken breast holds its shape. Dredge each chicken breast in flour, then in egg wash, and then in bread crumbs. Shake off excess and sauté in 2 oz of butter. Place the chicken in a baking pan and bake in the oven for 15 or 20 minutes or until the cheese starts to melt out of the chicken. To make the sauce, place butter, white wine, lemon pepper, lemon juice, roux, and garlic in a heavy sauce pot. Stir over a medium flame until the sauce thickens. Stir in heavy cream, add the Parmesan cheese and parsley, and pour over the chicken.

Mending nets at Railroad Wharf, Provincetown, c. 1915
PHOTO: GEORGE ELMER BROWNE

Squid

A dozen years ago, squid (also known as calamari or inkfish) was rarely seen outside of Italian and Asian neighborhoods, but today it's common in seafood markets and on restaurant menus now that the general public has accepted this versatile seafood, until quite recently considered "trash fish."

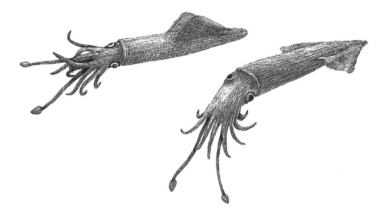

Squid is an excellent choice of food—it is highly nutritious, low in fat (less than 1%), inexpensive, and plentiful. In fact, the only problem with squid is cleaning it, a messy job, and time consuming (or as a local wag maintains, "It's easy, just ask someone who's never done it!"). But just as the average home cook these days would never gut and clean a fish, neither should we worry about having to clean a squid in order to eat it. Cleaned fresh squid is available in season at most coastal fish markets, and frozen in supermarkets throughout the country. It freezes very well and can be defrosted without any loss of flavor or texture. In fact, freezing is said to tenderize squid.

Squid has a sweet, nutty taste which makes it versatile to cook—it can be fried, stuffed, stewed and sautéed without losing its distinctive flavor. But a word of caution about cooking squid: it cooks quickly, like most shellfish, but when overcooked it becomes tough, and only prolonged cooking retenderizes it. An old saying goes: "Cook squid for 20 seconds or 2 hours."

Squid is a favorite food of striped bass and bluefish. Often these predatory game fish will drive large schools of them into harbors around the Cape. The squid can be so traumatized that they'll jump right out of the water onto the beach, where sharp-eyed folks are ready waiting with their fish buckets.

Sperm whales also include squid in their diet and it is the beak of the squid that causes ambergris to form in a whale's belly—the beak creates an irritation in the intestines and a gray, waxy substance forms around it. This is sometimes vomited up by the whale, and early whalers discovered that this substance, which they found floating on the surface of the ocean, formed a stable base for expensive perfumes, so it became much sought after. In fact, certain New England whaling captains made their fortunes from ambergris. In Provincetown, there's a plaque on an historic home where David C. Stull the "Ambergris King" lived. It is said that virtually all of the American ambergris collected in the 25-year period before his death in 1926 passed through his hands, at a time when the finest quality could fetch up to $350 a pound in Paris.

Small bone squid are found in Cape waters in the spring and early summer, particularly in Nantucket Sound. Squid are a valuable catch and a good squid year will boost a fisherman's annual income considerably. The larger summer squid arrive in late August and September and can be found as late as the early winter. When buying fresh squid at your local fish market, check that the flesh is purple-to-white, with a shiny skin and sweet smell. Squid are equally good stuffed whole, cut into rings and deep-fried, or simmered in an aromatic Portuguese squid stew—the following recipes give plenty of opportunity for adventure.

Sautéed Squid

This recipe, from the Lobster Pot Restaurant in Provincetown, is a quick and tasty way to prepare squid.

SERVES 4 AS AN APPETIZER.

1 lb squid, cleaned and cut into rings

2 oz butter

4 tablespoons olive oil

1 large clove garlic, crushed

2 small bay leaves

1 oz white wine

4 oz diced tomatoes

1 oz diced scallions

1 pinch crushed red pepper

Heat oil and butter in a sauté pan and sauté the garlic for a few minutes. Add the squid, tomatoes, scallions, wine, and seasonings and sauté until the squid is cooked *al dente*, about 3 or 4 minutes. Do NOT overcook. This dish may be served hot or cold.

Calamari Marinara

SERVES 4

1 lb squid, cleaned and cut into bite-sized pieces
1½ cups heavy cream
a pinch of oregano
a pinch of basil
white pepper to taste
1 clove garlic, crushed
1 cup freshly-made marinara sauce

Pour the heavy cream into a sauté pan with the oregano, basil, white pepper, and garlic. Heat over a medium flame, stirring constantly, to reduce the cream until it turns light yellow and thickens. Stir in the marinara sauce and squid. Heat over a medium flame until the calamari is just cooked, about 4 minutes. Taste the squid a few times to test if it is cooked. Remove from the heat the minute it is done. Serve immediately over your favorite pasta.

Squid Pie

This recipe comes from Jackson Lambert, an artist and humorist who lives in Provincetown.

SERVES 6	THESE QUANTITIES ARE APPROXIMATE:
	12 medium-sized local squid
	2 tablespoons olive oil
	1 cup chopped onion
	2 garlic cloves, crushed
	2 cups diced potatoes
	1 can tomatoes
	1/2 glass red wine
	dash of Worcestershire sauce
	1 teaspoon allspice
	salt and pepper to taste
	1 tablespoon flour
	pastry for a two-crust pie

Clean the squid (this is an easy task; just ask anyone who has never done it). Cut the flesh into 3/4" squares and the tentacles into one-inch strands, saving the largest head entire.

Sauté the onions and garlic in the olive oil in a large pot. When the onions are soft, add the squid, potatoes, tomatoes, red wine, allspice, salt, pepper, and Worcestershire sauce. Boil for 25 minutes. You may have to add some water along the way. At the end, add some flour to thicken the combination.

Line a deep pie dish with the pastry, pour in the squid mixture, cover with a top crust, and punch a few air holes in it.

Take the set-aside squid head, embed it firmly in the center of the top crust, and bake in a medium oven until the crust is well browned and the exposed head is tender. If this were a Portuguese dish, it might be called *Lula Torta*.

Squid Stew

4 to 6 large squid
2 medium onions, chopped
1/4 cup olive oil
1 cup crushed Italian tomatoes
1 clove garlic, crushed
1/2 cup chopped mushrooms
1 green pepper, chopped
1 cup red wine
a pinch of hot pepper flakes
pinch of oregano
1 bay leaf
salt and pepper to taste
chopped parsley

Clean the squid and wash them thoroughly. Cut the meat into thin strips. Remove the two longest tentacles and discard. Keep washing the squid until the meat is all white. Cut the bodies crosswise into rings about 1/4" wide. Separate the tentacles into bite-size pieces. Pat dry and set aside.

Lightly brown the chopped onion in olive oil. Add the garlic, hot peppers, bay leaf, oregano, and green pepper. Let mixture simmer and add more oil if it gets too dry. When the vegetables have softened, add the squid and stir until the squid becomes opaque, about one or two minutes. Add the red wine and mushrooms. Simmer until the squid starts turning color. Stir in the crushed tomatoes and cook for about 15 minutes. You may need to add water if the stew is too thick. To serve, remove the bay leaf and ladle into soup bowls; garnish with chopped parsley.

Portuguese Squid Stew

SERVES 6

24 squid, cleaned and sliced into rounds

1 quart water or fish stock

1 quart red wine

3 tablespoons olive oil

2 bay leaves

1 can diced tomatoes

2 tablespoons chopped parsley

1 onion, chopped

1 green pepper, chopped

6 cloves garlic, chopped

3 potatoes, diced

salt and pepper to taste

1 teaspoon ground allspice

1 tablespoon Worcestershire sauce

pinch of red pepper flakes to taste

Pour oil into a large pot and gently cook the onions, garlic, and chopped vegetables. Add all the seasonings with the water and wine and bring to a boil. Simmer for 1 hour. Add the squid, heat to boiling, and lower heat to a simmer. Simmer for 1½ hours, stirring occasionally. Add more liquid as needed. Serve with crusty Portuguese bread and a robust red wine.

Squid Orientale

This prize-winning recipe, speedy and economical, comes from the CAPE COD SEAFEST RECIPE SAMPLER.

SERVES 4

4 cleaned squid, cut into strips

3 tablespoons canola or sesame oil

2 medium onions, sliced

1 clove garlic or shallot, crushed

2 green peppers, chopped

2 stalks celery, chopped

3 ripe tomatoes, chopped

1 lb fresh mushrooms, sliced

1/4 small cabbage, thinly sliced

1 teaspoon oregano

pinch of basil and thyme

1 tablespoon tamari or soy sauce

a few pieces of dulse (optional)

Heat canola or sesame oil in a wok. Sauté squid quickly over high heat for about 8 minutes, stirring frequently. Transfer squid to a separate plate and set aside in a warm place.

Stir-fry the onion, garlic, peppers, and celery in the same oil until just tender. Add the cabbage slices and cook until tender. Add the chopped tomatoes and mushrooms and cook for a minute. Season to taste with tamari or soy sauce; add oregano, basil and thyme. When the vegetables are cooked but still a little on the firm side, add the cooked squid and heat through quickly, stirring all the while. Toss in dulse (a purple seaweed) if desired and heat through. Serve over a bed of rice.

Squid à la Plancha

Flavorful and unusual, this is a speedy dish to prepare.

SERVES 4

1 lb squid, cleaned and cut into pieces
2 tablespoons olive oil
1¹/₂ lbs shredded green cabbage
   (preferably Savoy)
2 cloves garlic, crushed
juice of one lemon
salt and pepper to taste
chopped parsley to garnish

Heat the olive oil in a heavy sauté pan over medium heat and stir-fry the cabbage. When it is just limp, add the garlic, salt and pepper and stir-fry for another 2 minutes. Remove to a platter and keep warm.

Heat a nonstick skillet over high heat until very hot, about 5 minutes. Sprinkle the bottom of the pan liberally with salt. Arrange squid in the pan but do not crowd (you may need to do this in two batches; salt the pan again before cooking the second batch.) Keep the heat up and cook for about 2 minutes, taking care not to burn the squid. Turn the squid over and cook the other side for one minute.

Arrange the squid on a serving platter on top of the cabbage and drizzle with lemon juice. Garnish with chopped parsley.

Fried Squid

A simple but effective recipe for fried squid. You may want to try coating the squid with beaten egg before dipping in seasoned flour for a richer flavor.

SERVES 8 AS
AN APPETIZER

2 lbs large whole squid

3 cups unbleached all-purpose flour

salt and pepper to taste

1 tablespoon baking soda

Clean squid and cut into 1/4" rings. Cut tentacles in half lengthwise if they are big. Shake off excess water and pat dry with kitchen towels. Best results are obtained when the squid is completely dry. Squid may be cleaned earlier in the day and refrigerated, wrapped in paper towels.

Preheat 3 or 4 inches of vegetable oil to 350 degrees. Season the flour to taste with salt and pepper and add the baking soda (baking soda makes the flour a golden brown when fried.) Toss the squid pieces in flour and shake well to remove the excess.

Test that oil is the right temperature with a small piece of bread—it should sizzle and turn golden brown, but not burn. Fry squid in hot oil until golden, about 2 to 3 minutes. Do not overcook. Drain on paper towels and serve immediately with tartar sauce or a dipping sauce of your choice.

Crunchy Squid Broil

Here is an easy recipe for broiling squid to perfection, so it is crisp and juicy, not tough and dry.

SERVES 4

**8 small squid with tentacles, cleaned
    and cut into rings**

1/2 cup powdered milk

GARLIC BUTTER:

1 oz butter

1 tablespoon minced garlic

2 oz creamed butter

a squeeze of lemon juice

salt and pepper to taste

Make the garlic butter by sautéing the minced garlic in 1 oz of butter until the garlic softens, 2 to 3 minutes. Do not let the garlic brown. Let cool a little and then mix the garlic with 2 oz of creamed butter. Season with salt, freshly-ground black pepper, and fresh lemon juice to taste.

Pat the squid dry and place in a shallow broiling pan. Dot with garlic butter. Then sprinkle powdered milk very lightly, but thoroughly, on the top side of the squid only. Place the pan under the broiler at the hottest setting. Broil until the squid turns a sizzling brown color— about 2 to 6 minutes, depending on the size of the squid and how hot the broiler gets. Serve immediately with cocktail or tartar sauce.

Josie's Italian Stuffed Squid

This is actually Josie's Italian grandmother's recipe. Josie, who lives in Harwich, recalls her grandmother serving this dish when her boyfriend first came to dinner with the family, back in the days before eating squid was considered something "normal" people did—but he soon abandoned his prejudices and acquired a taste for it, and apparently for Josie also, for they were married soon afterwards.

SERVES 6

12 small squid bodies, cleaned and left whole

1 pot freshly-made marinara sauce

STUFFING:

3 cups seasoned bread crumbs

1/4 cup chopped parsley

1/4 cup grated Parmesan cheese

1 clove garlic, crushed

1/4 cup olive oil

salt and pepper to taste

Mix the ingredients for the stuffing with olive oil and enough water to moisten and let the mixture sit while you clean and prepare the squid.

Make sure the squid are left whole so they will hold the filling without leaking. Fill each squid with stuffing and close the flap with a toothpick to keep the filling in place. Gently drop the stuffed squid into a pot of hot marinara sauce and cook at a low simmer for 20 or 30 minutes, enough time to allow the flavors to blend. Serve with plenty of marinara sauce and a robust red Italian wine.

Squid Stuffed with Spinach

SERVES 2 | **4 small squid, cleaned (retain tentacles)**
1 medium onion, chopped
2 tablespoons olive oil
1/2 cup chopped cooked spinach
1 beaten egg yolk
1/2 cup grated Swiss cheese
dash of nutmeg
salt and pepper to taste

Chop squid tentacles, then gently sauté the chopped onion and tentacles in 2 tablespoons of olive oil for about 10 minutes. Add the cooked spinach and cook for a few more minutes. Add the beaten egg yolk, the Swiss cheese, and season with salt and pepper and a dash of nutmeg. Stir the mixture to cook through, letting it cool slightly before stuffing the squid. Arrange the stuffed squid in an oiled baking dish and cover with tomato sauce. Bake in an oven at 450 degrees for 20 minutes.

Squid à la Muffler

From Howard Mitcham's PROVINCETOWN SEAFOOD COOKBOOK.

"Provincetown's fishermen are sometimes so busy with the fish that they don't have time to stop to fix lunch, so Captain John Santos and Vic Pacellini tell me they take small tender squids and lay them on the hot exhaust pipe and muffler of the boat's engine. In a few moments they are as brown and crisp as a potato chip. They eat them whole, feathers and all, spitting out the 'beak,' the hard mouth part of the squid."

Wellfleet Harbor

Shrimp

Shrimp as we generally know them are not native to the coast of New England, though a small pink shrimp is caught in these cold waters in December through February and represents the only fresh shrimp available in this area. They have a delicate, briny flavor and, because they are tiny, cook very quickly. Most of the shrimp found in the local markets is the warm-water shrimp, a versatile seafood. We eat more shrimp than any other fresh or frozen seafood (only canned tuna is more popular!) due to the fact that shrimp freeze extremely well and are therefore available all over the country.

About a quarter of our shrimp comes from the Gulf states, but the majority is imported, mostly from Asia, and Central and South America. About 80 percent of all imported shrimp is farm-raised, while much of the domestic catch is wild. Both farm-raised and wild shrimp can be flavorful, or insipid and mushy, depending on their diet—some farmed shrimp are raised on high-protein pellets, while others live in sealed bays where they get their nutrients from seawater, which can sometimes be nutritionally deficient.

There are three hundred species of shrimp world wide, but the types most commonly found in our markets are: Gulf shrimp, both white and pink—the most expensive and most flavorful—often caught wild; Gulf brown, a wild shrimp, less desirable than the white and pink, and likely to taste of iodine, due to the plankton on which they feed; Ecuadorian or Mexican white, similar to Gulf white, the most heavily imported shrimp in this country, though less flavorful; Chinese white, an inexpensive Asian farm-raised shrimp with a grayish white color, soft texture, and mild flavor; and the firm and flavorful Black Tiger, widely farmed in Asia, dark gray with black stripes and red feelers, but which turn pink when cooked.

Buy frozen shrimp rather than thawed, as thawed shrimp gives you no advantage over frozen, because who knows when it was defrosted? Defrosted shrimp also quickly lose their freshness in a few days while frozen shrimp stored in the freezer will retain their quality for several weeks. Always purchase shrimp with the shells on; cleaning before freezing will deprive shrimp of some of their flavor and texture. Shrimp should have no black spots on them; this is a sign that a breakdown of their flesh has begun. They should smell of saltwater and little else, and when thawed, should be firm and fill the shell fully. The flavor and texture of shrimp can be improved by letting them sit in a brine for 2 hours or so before cooking. Dissolve a cup of salt and half a cup of sugar in 2 cups of boiling water. Pour this into a large bowl filled with ice and water, enough to cover up to 2 pounds of shrimp. Refrigerate, adding more ice if needed.

Shrimp cook in as little as 3 minutes and will turn pink when done— their flavor and texture is seriously impaired by overcooking. If possible, leave the shells on while cooking; the shrimp taste better, though eating them is messier. The smaller local New England shrimp are pink when raw and cook in one minute; they are best steamed with their shells on.

Shrimp & Scallop Seviche

A succulent appetizer from the elegant Regatta restaurant, in two locations, at Cotuit and Falmouth. The acid in the vinegar, wine and lemon juice "cooks" the seafood.

SERVES 4

8 oz raw shrimp, deveined and shelled

8 oz sea scallops, quartered

1 small red onion, chopped

1 large green pepper, chopped

1 cup olive oil

1/4 cup wine vinegar

1/4 cup white wine

1/4 cup fresh lemon juice

salt and white pepper to taste

1 bay leaf

a pinch of chopped thyme, chervil and basil

Place shrimp, scallops, and chopped vegetables in a stainless steel bowl. To make the marinade, put the remaining ingredients in a heavy pot and bring to a boil. Pour the boiling marinade over the seafood, toss and let stand at room temperature until cooled. Refrigerate for 24 hours. Stir occasionally to make sure all the seafood is covered with marinade.

To serve, remove seafood with a slotted spoon and arrange on a bed of Boston lettuce. Garnish with a cherry tomato, lemon or lime wedges, and a sprig of fresh dill.

Insalata di Scampi e Carciofi

A simple but appealing appetizer of shrimp and artichoke hearts from Ciro Cozzi of Ciro & Sal's Italian Restaurant in Provincetown.

SERVES 6 TO 8 | 1 lb raw shrimp
1 15-oz can artichoke hearts
juice of 1 lemon
2 tablespoons olive oil
1 teaspoon fresh mint, finely chopped
  or 1/2 teaspoon dry mint
1 teaspoon parsley, finely chopped
salt and pepper to taste

Place shrimp in a saucepan and pour in enough water to cover them. Place a lid on the pan and boil the shrimp in their shells for 5 minutes. Do not overcook. Drain the shrimp and let them cool a little. Shell the shrimp and cut into 1/8" slices.

Drain the artichoke hearts and chop them coarsely. Mix all the other ingredients in a bowl, add the shrimp and artichoke hearts, and chill. Allow to stand for at least a half hour before serving.

Note: shrimp are more juicy and flavorful when cooked in their shells.

Ciro's Scampi alla Griglia

Another delicious shrimp dish, decadently swimming in butter and garlic, from Ciro & Sal's in Provincetown.

SERVES 4

28 large shrimp, shelled and deveined
6 scallions
1¹/₃ cups clarified butter (recipe on page 89)
2/3 cup olive oil
2 large garlic cloves, peeled and chopped
2 small onions, finely chopped
juice of one lemon
salt and freshly ground black pepper

Preheat the broiler. Thinly slice the scallions, both white and green parts, on the diagonal. Combine the butter, oil, garlic, chopped onion, lemon juice, salt and pepper in a bowl and blend thoroughly with a whisk.

Arrange the shrimp in a shallow ovenproof pan and sprinkle the scallions over them. Pour the butter and oil mixture over the shrimp. Put the pan under the broiler, 3" from the heat source, and broil the shrimp for about 3 minutes on each side.

Transfer the shrimp to a warm serving dish, pour over the sauce, and serve immediately.

Baked Stuffed Shrimp

Here's a real Cape Cod classic—the recipe is Mildred Felton's, proprietor of The Cottage Restaurant in Provincetown during the 1960s and '70s, an old-time restaurant that dished up the best home-style food in town.

SERVES 4

16 jumbo Gulf shrimp

1 cup crabmeat, cut in small pieces

1/2 lb butter

1 large onion, chopped coarsely

2 ribs celery, chopped

1 tablespoon chopped green pepper (optional)

1/3 cup chopped parsley

2 cloves garlic, minced

1/2 teaspoon paprika

1/4 teaspoon chopped dill

dash cayenne pepper

1 cup chopped fresh mushrooms

1/4 cup dry white wine

2 cups dry bread crumbs or cracker crumbs

Sauté the onion, celery, green pepper, parsley and garlic in butter until the onion is tender and golden. Add paprika, dill, cayenne pepper, mushrooms, and wine. Mix in the bread or cracker crumbs until the mixture holds together. Gently mix in crabmeat so it doesn't break up too much. De-vein and butterfly each shrimp and "stuff" with stuffing mixture. Arrange the shrimp in a baking pan or in individual serving dishes. Dot with butter and bake in the oven at 450 degrees for 20 to 25 minutes. Do not overcook or the shrimp will become dry.

For a gourmet feast, top with Newburg Sauce (recipe on page 100).

Shrimp in Pesto Cream Sauce

SERVES 4

32 medium shrimp, shelled and de-veined

2 tablespoons butter

1 cup flour

2 tablespoons finely diced onion

1/2 pint heavy cream, more if you prefer

1 lb pasta of your choice

PESTO SAUCE:

5 cups fresh basil leaves

3 cloves garlic

1/2 cup pine nuts, or chopped walnuts

1/2 cup chopped Italian parsley leaves

1/2 to 1 cup olive oil

1 teaspoon salt

1/2 cup freshly-grated Parmesan cheese

To make the pesto sauce, place all the ingredients in a blender or food processor and blend the mixture until smooth, adding more oil if needed.

Cook the pasta in a large pot of boiling water until *al dente*.

Meanwhile, lightly dredge the shrimp in flour and sauté them in butter in a skillet over medium heat. Allow about 2 minutes per side. Add the chopped onion when one side of the shrimp has cooked, and continue sautéing for a further 2 minutes. Add the heavy cream and bring to a slow simmer, just long enough for the cream to heat through. Do not overcook the shrimp. Add one cup of pesto sauce to the shrimp and mix in thoroughly.

Drain pasta into a serving dish, pour pesto cream sauce over the pasta, and serve immediately.

Gulf Shrimp in Phyllo with Caviar Beurre Blanc

This elegant recipe comes from Ocean Edge Resort in Brewster.

SERVES 4 AS AN APPETIZER

4 large Gulf shrimp

4 sheets of phyllo dough

1 oz melted butter

1 cup heavy cream

1 tablespoon minced shallots

1 tablespoon champagne vinegar

4 oz butter, softened

4 oz caviar

Peel and de-vein the shrimp. Brush 4 sheets of phyllo dough with melted butter and stack them one on top of each other. Cut dough into 1" strips and wrap up each shrimp, leaving the tail exposed. Place on a baking sheet and bake at 350 degrees for 5 to 7 minutes until the pastry is brown. Remove from the oven and keep warm while you make the beurre blanc.

Heat the heavy cream in a saucepan with shallots and champagne vinegar. Reduce by half. Beat in 4 oz butter until it is well mixed. Keep the sauce warm until ready to serve.

To serve, place one shrimp on each serving plate and cover with a spoonful of beurre blanc. Add a dollop of caviar just before serving.

Barbecued Shrimp & Scallops Oriental

1 lb large shrimp

1 lb sea scallops

3/4 cup soy sauce

1/2 cup sesame or peanut oil

1 bunch scallions, minced

2 teaspoons ground or minced fresh ginger

2 tablespoons brown sugar

Light a charcoal fire. Peel and de-vein the shrimp, leaving on the tails. Cut the scallops in half if they are very large, otherwise leave them whole. Make a marinade of the soy sauce, oil, scallions, ginger and brown sugar, mixing well. Marinate the shrimp and scallops in this mixture for at least 4 hours, turning frequently. Thread shrimp and scallops alternately on skewers, leaving a little space between each. Broil over hot coals until done. Serve with fragrant Basmati rice and top with any remaining marinade if you wish.

Pasta with Shrimp al Olio

SERVES 4

32 medium shrimp
6 anchovy fillets, chopped
1 or 2 cloves garlic, chopped
1/2 cup olive oil
flour for dredging
1/2 cup clam juice
1/2 cup white wine
freshly ground black pepper to taste
1/2 cup Parmesan cheese
1 lb pasta of your choice

Peel and de-vein the shrimp. Chop the garlic and anchovies. Heat the olive oil in a large skillet. Dredge the shrimp in flour, shake off the excess, and sauté in the skillet for a minute or 2 on each side. Add the chopped garlic and anchovies, and sauté for a few more minutes until the garlic just starts to turn golden brown. Stir in the white wine and clam juice and bring to a boil. Remove skillet from the heat and add a dash of pepper to taste. Stir in half a cup of Parmesan cheese, freshly grated if possible, and serve immediately over pasta.

Shrimp & Scallop Sauté

SERVES 4

16 medium shrimp
8 sea scallops, halved or quartered
2 oz butter
1 clove garlic, minced or crushed
pinch of thyme
1 cup chopped parsley
salt and pepper to taste
3 tablespoons heavy cream
dash of lemon juice
dash of paprika

Melt butter in a heavy pan and add garlic, thyme, chopped parsley, salt and pepper. Sauté for a few minutes until the garlic is soft. Add the shrimp and scallops and sauté for 5 or 6 minutes, stirring briskly. Stir in the heavy cream. Lower the heat, add a dash of lemon juice, and stir just a few times. Serve on a warmed platter, topped with a little chopped parsley and a sprinkling of paprika. Accompany with steamed rice.

Shrimp Bombay

This is the recipe for my favorite dish at the Arbor Restaurant in Orleans.

SERVES 2

8 medium shrimp

1 10-oz boneless chicken breast,
    cut into long strips

1/4 cup olive oil

1 clove garlic, finely chopped

1 apple, thinly sliced

2 oz dark raisins

1/2 cup curry sauce

3 tablespoons roux (flour and butter mix)

3 cups light cream

2 cups cooked brown rice

coconut shreds and chopped almonds to garnish

Heat the olive oil in a heavy pan. Sauté the chicken and garlic in hot oil for a few minutes. Add the shrimp, apples, and raisins and sauté over low heat for a few minutes. Stir in the curry sauce and then mix in the roux. Turn up the heat a little, stir in the cream and simmer for about 20 minutes.

Spoon about a cup of cooked brown rice into each of two individual casserole dishes and pour curry mixture on top. Sprinkle sautéed coconut shreds and chopped almonds on top and bake in an oven at 350 degrees for about 10 minutes before serving.

Shrimp Feta

This flavorful shrimp dish, which originated in the Greek islands, comes from Napi's in Provincetown. The shrimp are sauteed in butter, flamed with Ouzo and Metaxa brandy, then baked with a sauce of tomatoes topped with feta cheese.

SERVES 2

1 lb medium-sized shrimp

1 tablespoon Ouzo

1 tablespoon Metaxa brandy

4 tablespoons crumbled feta cheese

4 tablespoons butter

THE SAUCE:

1 lb fresh tomatoes, peeled, seeded
   and chopped

1 medium-sized onion, diced

2 cloves garlic, diced

2 tablespoons chopped fresh parsley

1/2 teaspoon basil

1/4 teaspoon oregano

salt and pepper to taste

To make the sauce, sauté the onion and garlic with a little olive oil in a skillet until translucent. Add the tomatoes and herbs. Gently cook together until the flavors have blended—at least 30 minutes, but the longer the better. Once the sauce is made this dish proceeds quickly.

Meanwhile, peel the shrimp. Melt the butter in a skillet and sauté the shrimp briefly on each side until they begin to turn pink. Add the Ouzo and brandy and flame them. Allow the shrimp to cook until the flames die away.

Spoon the shrimp into an ovenproof dish and pour the Ouzo/brandy sauce on top. Spoon a thin layer of tomato sauce over the shrimp, and crumble the feta cheese on top. Carefully place the dish under a broiler for a few minutes to brown the cheese, and serve immediately.

Creamed Scampi

Another delightful recipe from Astrid Berg, chef at Pepe's Wharf seafood restaurant in Provincetown.

SERVES 6

48 medium shrimp, peeled and de-veined

1/2 cup clarified butter (see recipe on page 89)

THE SAUCE:

1 tablespoon butter

3 tablespoons flour

1 pint heavy cream

2 cloves garlic, finely minced

1/2 cup dry white wine

salt and pepper to taste

juice of a lemon

1 tomato, seeded, peeled, and diced medium

Melt the butter in a skillet and add the flour to make a roux. Add heavy cream a little at a time, whisking in well to prevent lumps. Add the garlic. Stir in the white wine and lemon juice and season to taste. Continue cooking, stirring all the while, until the mixture thickens. Add the diced tomato last and just heat through—do not cook it.

In another skillet, sauté the shrimp for a few minutes on both sides in clarified butter until they just turn pink (do not overcook). Remove the shrimp from the skillet with a slotted spoon and arrange on a serving platter. Pour sauce over shrimp and serve with rice or pasta.

Gambas a la Plancha

This recipe was adapted by Truro summer resident Ray Elman from a dish served at El Charro in New York City. It's wonderfully flavorful, a speedy dish to serve at a dinner party—one of my favorites.

SERVES 4

32 medium-sized shrimp, in the shell

3 tablespoons olive oil

5 garlic cloves, squeezed through a press

1 jalapeño pepper, chopped

handful of chopped parsley

juice of one lemon

1/3 cup dry white wine

4 tablespoons dry sherry

1 4-oz can Old El Paso taco sauce

paprika

Use a wok or a deep frying pan that will fit under the broiler. You also need a lid large enough to cover the wok or pan. Preheat the broiler.

Over a medium flame, heat the pan and add the olive oil. Add the crushed garlic and sauté for one minute. Add the jalapeño pepper and continue to sauté until the garlic is golden. Add the parsley, stirring continuously.

Add the shrimp, continue stirring for 20 seconds, then stir in the lemon juice, taco sauce, sherry, and white wine. Cover the entire mixture with a liberal sprinkling of paprika, then put a lid on the pan. Cook for exactly 2 minutes, remove the lid, and place the pan under the broiler. Cook for another 2 minutes, and it's done. Serve over saffron rice.

Preparing salt cod in Provincetown, c. 1915.
PHOTO: GEORGE ELMER BROWNE

Fishing for Compliments:
Seafood Stews & Medleys

This chapter contains some of the most delicious recipes ever invented, dishes that combine the fruits of the sea in heavenly combinations. While some are native to New England shores, most of them are classics from other cultures, but the seafood that abounds off Cape Cod may be perfectly adapted to virtually any fish dish.

The classic seafood stews all have one thing in common: they are made basically with a seasoned stock in which is simmered a variety of fish. They differ little in technique, but widely in the seasonings and types of fish used. French bouillabaisse, for example, is a mess of fish cooked in a garlicky tomato-based broth; it can be served with *rouille*, a traditional accompaniment, or with *aioli*, when it is called "bourride."

Zarzuela, the classic Catalonian mixed shellfish dish, is a little more spicy, usually containing saffron and chili or hot peppers, and is not so much a stew as a plate of fish covered with broth; while paella, the national dish of Spain, is a rice dish simmered in fish stock, topped with a melange of seafood, chicken, and sausage. Cioppino, the Italian answer to bouillabaisse, depends on olive oil, tomatoes, and red wine for its hearty flavor. Some of these dishes require fish stock in their preparation, so the first recipe in this chapter is for a basic but flavorful stock. When a recipe calls for clams or mussels, the broth from steaming the shellfish can also be used as stock.

The types of fish traditionally used in these dishes are native to the region of origin, so a cioppino from the Adriatic or bouillabaisse from Marseilles will taste totally different from one prepared on Cape Cod. With this in mind, local cooks can be creative; they can pretty much throw in anything they can lay their hands on, so long as the fish is white and firm-fleshed, not dark and oily like mackerel or tuna. The greater the variety of seafood, the more robust the broth—and the more flavorful the basic stock used, the better the final dish will be. Simmering shellfish with their shells on also adds flavor to the stew; a little messier to eat maybe, but more fun.

Unlike meat stews, fish stews are rarely better when reheated. The fish and seafood can be cleaned and trimmed and the sauce or stock pre-pared in advance, but the marriage of the two must be left until the last possible moment. The stew must be served up when the fish is perfectly cooked and still recognizable. Any later and the fish will begin to flake and disintegrate. When a recipe calls for many different species of fish and shellfish, it often means staggering their entry into the stock and carefully timing the cooking.

Keep side dishes simple. Since practically all fish stews require last-minute attention, there's no point in complicating the chef's life more than necessary. Most fish stews are meal enough in themselves and don't need additional vegetables. Opt for plenty of fresh bread, garlic bread, or croutons, and a large salad of crisp greens.

Basic Fish Stock

MAKES ABOUT
3 PINTS **2 to 3 lbs fish bones and trimmings from
any white fish (do not use dark fish such
as mackerel and bluefish)**

1 pint white wine

1 leek, sliced

1 large carrot, sliced

1/2 stalk celery, sliced

2 stalks parsley

1 bay leaf

1 tablespoon white wine vinegar

8 black peppercorns

3 pints water

Put all the ingredients into a large pan and bring to a boil. Skim off the surface and simmer gently for 20 minutes. Do not simmer any longer or the stock may develop a bitter taste. Strain the the stock before using.

Fish stock freezes well, in case you have any left over. A useful way to freeze stock is in ice cube trays, especially for recipes that call for a small quantity of stock.

Bouillabaisse à la Cape Cod

A lot has been written about preparing an authentic bouillabaisse, but like many noted dishes, it depends more on fresh ingredients than on superior culinary skills for its unqualified success. The secret to a good bouillabaisse is a rich fish stock and a variety of fresh seafood, where the more "trashy" the fish, the more flavorful will be the stew. Any firm-fleshed white fish will do, but use whole fish cut into chunks, not fillets, which will disintegrate. And never use dark, oily fish, which will spoil the flavor and color of the stew. Halibut, cod, sea bass, haddock, monkfish, skate wings, squid, whiting, butterfish, hake—all these will add to the complex flavors of a magnificent bouillabaisse.

SERVES 8

Saffron may be added to this dish as an optional ingredient.

2 lbs mixed fresh, firm-fleshed white fish, cut into chunks

24 littleneck clams, well scrubbed

24 mussels, well scrubbed with beards removed

24 oysters, well scrubbed

24 medium shrimp in their shells

16 sea scallops, halved

1/2 cup olive oil

1/2 cup finely chopped onion

6 cloves garlic, minced

4 leeks, white portions only, finely chopped

4 cups fish stock

4 fresh tomatoes, skinned

1 tablespoon chopped fresh fennel

1 teaspoon crushed saffron

2 bay leaves, crushed

1 teaspoon grated orange rind

2 tablespoons tomato paste

1/4 teaspoon celery or fennel seed

3 tablespoons chopped fresh parsley

1 teaspoon ground white pepper

salt to taste

ROUILLE:

6 cloves garlic

1 egg yolk

a teaspoon salt

dash of Tabasco

1 teaspoon dried oregano or
  12 large basil leaves

1 cup olive oil

1/3 cup canned red pimientos

1/3 cup fresh non-sweet bread crumbs

Heat the oil in a large sauté pot with a tight-fitting lid and sauté the onion and garlic until transparent. Add the leeks and sauté until soft. Add the fish stock to the pan and then the other ingredients, except the fish and shellfish. Cook, stirring, until the aroma of the spices is redolent in the air. Turn down to a simmer and cook for about 10 minutes.

Meanwhile, make the *rouille* by blending all the ingredients, except the oil, in a food processor. When well blended, gradually add the oil in a light stream with the processor on low until the *rouille* takes on the consistency of mayonnaise. Serve at room temperature.

Now add the clams to the broth and cook, covered, for 5 minutes. Add the mussels and fish to the broth and cook another for 5 minutes. When the first of the clams begins to open, add the remaining shellfish. (You may like to add a tablespoon of Pernod or Pastis at this point for a real Mediterranean flavor.) Cover the pot and cook for 3 to 5 minutes, shaking the pot a few times to help open the shells. Remove any shellfish that have not opened and serve immediately in soup plates with homemade croutons as a garnish, topped with a dollop of *rouille*.

This dish was developed in Marseilles by fishermen's wives as a way of utilizing fish that was usually discarded. Traditionally, the broth is served first as a soup course and the fish as a second course.

Zuppa di Pesce

This dish—literally "fish soup"— is considered very festive in Italy.
In many places this is a traditional dish served on Christmas Eve.

SERVES 6

12 littleneck clams, well scrubbed

12 mussels, well scrubbed, beards removed

1/2 lb scallops

1 lobster, cut up (about 1½ lbs)

1/2 lb medium-sized shrimp

1 lb firm-fleshed fish, e.g. cod or haddock, cut up

1/4 cup olive oil

6 cloves garlic, minced

1 small onion, finely chopped

a pinch of oregano, basil and rosemary

1 bay leaf

3/4 cup dry white wine

1 large can whole tomatoes, crushed by hand

salt and pepper to taste

Heat the olive oil in a deep pot and sauté the garlic and onion until transparent. Add the shellfish and seasonings and stir well. Add the white wine and raise the heat under the pot so that most of the wine evaporates. Cook like this for about 4 minutes, stirring all the time.

Lower the heat and add the crushed tomatoes. Add the fish and stir gently. Cover the pot and steam for about 5 or 6 minutes. All the shellfish should have opened by this time. Serve in deep soup bowls over linguine, or pour over thick slices of toasted Italian bread.

Cioppino

This dish proves the theory that much of the world's greatest cooking is actually the simplest, depending in the main on high quality fresh ingredients. Here is Ciro Cozzi's version of the classic Italian seafood stew.

SERVES 10-12

1 striped bass or sea bass, 6 or 8 lbs

1 lb medium-sized shrimp

32 mussels

32 littleneck clams

1 2-lb lobster

4 squids and their tentacles, cleaned and diced

3 or 4 tomatoes

2 green peppers

1/2 cup olive oil

10 scallions, chopped

2 cloves garlic, minced

2 tablespoons chopped parsley

2 cups dry red wine

dash of red wine vinegar

salt and pepper to taste

Clean the fish and cut into several pieces. Shell and de-vein the shrimp, and leave the tails on. Scrub the mussels and clams thoroughly. Cut the lobster into pieces. Peel and chop the tomatoes and green peppers.

Heat the olive oil in a deep pot and add the scallions, garlic, and peppers. Sauté for five minutes. Add the tomatoes and cook for 15 more minutes. Add the wine and allow the vegetables to cook slowly for an additional 20 minutes, stirring occasionally. Add the fish and shellfish, cover tightly, and cook gently until the clams open. Stir in the chopped parsley, a dash of red wine vinegar, and salt and pepper to taste. Serve steaming hot in preheated soup bowls with garlic bread.

Paella

When cooked properly, paella is one of the most delicious of the great seafood dishes of the world, native to Spain, and named after the pan in which it is cooked. This is a scaled down version of the more complicated and time-consuming classic, easy to make in the average kitchen with ingredients readily available on the Cape. The secret to a successful paella is to have plenty of flavorful clam broth to cook the rice in. A dry, tasteless paella is a most disappointing dish.

SERVES 6

8 chicken legs, jointed

12 littleneck clams, scrubbed

12 mussels, well scrubbed, beards removed

12 shrimp, peeled and de-veined

3 or 4 small squid, cleaned and cut into pieces

1/2 cup flour

6 tablespoons olive oil

1 cup white wine

1 large onion, diced

3 garlic cloves, chopped

2 whole garlic cloves, unpeeled

1 pinch saffron

3 cups white rice

4 hot Italian sausages, sliced into 1/2" medallions

1 cup chopped fresh tomatoes

Heat olive oil in a large, wide pan. Flour the chicken pieces, shake off the excess, and sauté in oil until lightly browned on all sides. Reduce heat and cook until chicken is cooked through—about 20 minutes. Remove from pan and keep warm.

In a separate pot with a tight-fitting lid, steam the clams and mussels in white wine with 2 whole garlic cloves until most of the shells have opened. Do not overcook the shellfish. Discard any that do not open. Drain and keep warm. Strain and reserve the broth.

Cook the diced onion and chopped garlic in olive oil in the same pan used to cook the chicken. Sauté gently until the onions are translucent. Add the saffron and clam broth. Add the rice and bring to a boil. Simmer slowly, uncovered, until the rice is almost cooked. Add more broth or water if the liquid simmers away too fast. The rice should absorb the broth and cook in approximately 20 minutes.

Meanwhile, sauté the sausage pieces in a separate skillet until cooked. Add the sausage and the tomatoes to the rice and stir in. Do not let the mixture get too dry; add more broth if necessary. Add the squid with the tentacles and cook, stirring gently for 5 minutes longer, and then stir in the shrimp. Cook for 3 or 4 minutes or until the shrimp is just done and turns pink. To serve, spoon rice mixture into large soup plates, arranging chicken and seafood on top. For a real Cape Cod feast, you may wish to add a couple of steamed lobsters.

Quahog Boats at Rock Harbor, Orleans, 1916   POSTCARD COURTESY OF NOEL W. BEYLE

Zarzuela

In Spain a "zarzuela" is a comic operetta and the fish stew of the same name is a happy mixture of several different varieties of fish and shellfish, cooked with a saffron and chili-flavored tomato sauce. Though not a dish that can be made in 30 minutes, this recipe is not so onerous to cook because much can be made ready in advance. The mussels can be steamed, fish trimmed, and the sauce half-cooked several hours before you need them. The whole cast needs to assemble only half an hour or so before the curtain is due to rise.

SERVES 6

1 lb fresh squid plus tentacles, cleaned and
   cut into small rings

24 small mussels, scrubbed

12 oysters, scrubbed

12 oz monkfish, cut into 1½" cubes
   (reserve any trimmings)

12 oz hake or other firm-fleshed white fish cut
   into steaks 1" thick (reserve any trimmings)

1/2 lb medium shrimp

6 jumbo shrimp

8 oz cooked lobster meat, cut into chunks
   (optional)

generous pinch saffron threads

1/2 cup olive oil

1 onion, finely chopped

3 cloves garlic, chopped

1 lb tomatoes, skinned, deseeded
   and roughly chopped

1 bay leaf

1 teaspoon paprika

1 small dried red chili, deseeded

1 pint white wine

salt and pepper

2 tablespoons chopped parsley

Remove shells from half of the medium shrimp and reserve shells. Heat 1/2" of water in a pan with a tight fitting lid and steam the mussels over high heat until they open. Discard any that do not open. Drain well and strain the cooking broth through a sieve lined with muslin or kitchen paper. Return the broth to the pan, together with shrimp shells and any fish trimmings. Add water to cover if necessary and bring to the boil. Simmer for 20 minutes. Strain and reserve the stock.

Soak the saffron in 2 tablespoons of warm water. Heat the olive oil in a wide, shallow flameproof casserole. Add onion and garlic and cook gently until soft and golden, a good 10 minutes. Raise heat slightly and add the tomatoes, bay leaf, paprika, and chili. Cook until very thick. Stir in the saffron and its water, the white wine and about a cup of the stock, plus salt and pepper. Bring to a simmer and taste for seasoning.

Then add the fish to the stock in the reverse order of how quickly they cook. First the monkfish: simmer, uncovered, for 5 minutes; then the hake and the jumbo shrimp and simmer for another 5 minutes. Add the oysters and cook, covered, for another 5 minutes. Then add the squid and medium shrimp and cook for a few more minutes. When the squid is opaque and the shrimp just turn pink, add the cooked mussels in their shells and the cooked lobster meat, and heat though for a few more minutes. Serve in the casserole, or transfer to a warm serving dish, and sprinkle with chopped parsley.

Jagaçita or Portuguese Paella

This is a wonderful recipe I adapted from one given to me by Tony and Elspeth Vevers of Provincetown, who got it from Maurice Lopes in 1955 during their first winter on the Cape. There's something about the combination of linguiça and steamed clams that's absolutely irresistible—and this dish is especially impressive when served at a dinner party topped with a steamed lobster.

SERVES 6

1 cup white rice

1 lb linguiça (Portuguese sausage)
   cut into 1/4" slices

2 or 3 chicken breasts, separated into
   bite-sized pieces

12 littlenecks, well scrubbed

12 mussels, well scrubbed

2 medium onions, sliced

2 cloves garlic, crushed

1 red pepper, sliced

1 green pepper, sliced

Cook the rice until the grains are light and separated. Meanwhile, fry the linguiça in a large pan with a tightly-fitting lid. When cooked, remove the pieces with a slotted spoon and set aside in a warm place. Sauté the onions, garlic, and peppers in the remaining linguiça fat. When the vegetables are nearly limp, remove from the pan and set aside in a warm place. Brown the chicken in any remaining fat, adding a little olive oil if necessary. When cooked, combine all these ingredients with the cooked rice in the same large pot, stirring well. Add the clams and mussels and cover the pan. Cook gently until all the clams and mussels have opened and released their juice into the rice. Remove any shellfish that haven't opened. Ladle the rice mixture into large soup plates and arrange the shellfish and chicken on top. Serve with a tossed salad, Portuguese bread, and a hearty wine.

Seafood Stew with Native Corn & Basil

SERVES 2

4 medium shrimp

4 sea scallops, halved

1¼ lb lobster, cooked, with tail and
    claw meat removed

1 tablespoon olive oil

2 scallions, sliced thinly

2 Red Bliss potatoes, cut in half,
    and sliced 1/4" thick

1 cup fish stock or clam juice

1 cup heavy cream

5 basil leaves, chopped

1 ear fresh corn

1/2 small red pepper, julienned

1/2 small yellow pepper, julienned

Shuck the corn and cut off the kernels. Remove the shells from the shrimp. Heat the olive oil in a sauce pot and briefly cook the scallions and potatoes for 30 seconds. Add the clam juice and simmer until the potatoes are just cooked. Add the cream, corn, shrimp, scallops, lobster meat, basil, and red and yellow peppers. Simmer slowly until the seafood is just cooked through and the shrimp turn pink. Add salt and pepper to taste and serve immediately.

Bourride

CREAMY GARLIC FISH SOUP

This recipe was served at the Provincetown Center for Coastal Studies' first "Trash Fish Dinner" in 1979 by Molly O'Neill, at that time chef of the Café at the Mews in Provincetown. Readers of the NEW YORK TIMES will recognize Molly as the current food columnist for the SUNDAY TIMES MAGAZINE.

SERVES 6 TO 8

5 cups fish stock

2 cups aioli sauce

1 cup light cream

1/2 cup minced parsley

1/2 cup minced celery leaves

FISH STOCK:

5 lbs "trash" fish, the wider the variety the better

1 cup sliced carrots

1 cup sliced celery

6 tablespoons olive oil

8 cups white wine

8 cups water

a small bunch of parsley, coarsely chopped

1 tablespoon dried fennel

1 bay leaf

AIOLI SAUCE:

1 tablespoon minced parsley

12 cloves garlic, minced

4 egg yolks

1 tablespoon boiling water

1/2 teaspoon salt

freshly-ground pepper to taste

2 cups olive oil

1 tablespoon lemon juice

To make the stock, rinse the fish and gut any big ones. In a large stock pot, sauté the carrots and celery in olive oil until they just begin to turn color. Add 8 cups of white wine, 8 cups of water and the fish. Bring to a boil, skim, and add the parsley, fennel, and a bay leaf. Simmer for an hour. Strain the stock through cheese cloth, return to heat and reduce by half. Season to taste. Strain again through cheese cloth. Use as much stock as you need for this recipe, and freeze the rest in quart containers.

While the stock is simmering, make the aioli sauce. Place garlic and egg yolks in a mixer and whisk. Add a tablespoon of boiling water and season with salt and pepper. Then add olive oil drop-by-drop, mixing continuously, until more than half has been added and well incorporated. Then you may mix in the oil in increasing quantities. When all the oil has been added, beat in the lemon juice and parsley.

Warm 5 cups of the strained fish stock. Slowly whisk in 2 cups of aioli sauce into half of the stock. Stir this into the other half of the stock and heat, but do not boil or the eggs will scramble. Stir in one cup of light cream, add the minced parsley and celery leaves, and serve.

Baiting up trawl in Provincetown, c. 1920.   POSTCARD COURTESY OF NOEL W. BEYLE

Sesuit Stew-It

I came across this recipe—Cape Cod's cheap and easy answer to a bouillabaisse—in a booklet published in 1981 by the Cape Cod Seafood Council.

SERVES 6

2 lbs small quahogs, well scrubbed

2 lbs pollock, tautog or other white "trash" fish

3 tablespoons olive oil

1/2 cup butter

2 large onions, chopped

2 large green peppers, chopped

3 large tomatoes, chopped

1/2 cup white wine

1 clove garlic, minced

salt and pepper to taste

Cover the bottom of a Dutch oven with oil. Heat the oil and place the scrubbed quahogs in the pot. Place half the chopped onions, peppers, and tomatoes on top of the clams. Place half the fish over the vegetable mixture. Finish with a second layer of fish. Dot with butter and sprinkle with salt and pepper. Pour on the wine, cover, and bring to a boil; simmer gently for about 35 minutes. Serve in large soup plates, garnished with chopped parsley. Delicious!

Seafood Alberto

This recipe comes from one of my favorite restaurants, Alberto's in Hyannis.

SERVES 4

8 littleneck clams, well scrubbed

8 mussels, well scrubbed

8 large shrimp

8 sea scallops, halved

4 oz calamari, sliced

1 cup white wine

3 cloves garlic, minced

1/4 cup olive oil

MARINARA SAUCE:

1 cup chopped celery

1¹/₂ cups roughly-chopped carrots

3 cups roughly-chopped onions

3 cups crushed fresh tomatoes

1/4 cup olive oil

2 cloves garlic, minced

salt and pepper to taste

To prepare the sauce, purée the celery, carrots, and onions. Heat the oil in a sauce pot and sauté the purée for about 5 minutes. Add the minced garlic and salt and pepper to taste. Add the crushed tomatoes and simmer for at least an hour, stirring occasionally.

Meanwhile, steam the clams and mussels together in 1/4 cup olive oil and 1/2 cup of white wine in a pot with a tight fitting lid. Steam over medium heat, covered, until the shellfish have opened. Add the shrimp, scallops, calamari, and garlic to the pot and cook, stirring, for two minutes. Stir in 3 cups of marinara sauce and the remaining 1/2 cup of white wine. Reduce the sauce a little so it thickens, and serve over pasta.

Seafood Crêpe

This creamy crêpe recipe makes an unusual and elegant main course; from Astrid Berg, chef of Pepe's Wharf seafood restaurant in Provincetown.

SERVES 6

6 oz lobster meat

6 oz shrimp

6 oz crabmeat

1/2 cup clarified butter

CRÊPE BATTER:

1 cup all-purpose flour

pinch of salt

3 eggs

1 cup milk, more if needed

2 tablespoons melted butter

BÉCHAMEL SAUCE:

1 tablespoon butter

1 tablespoon flour

1 cup milk

pinch of nutmeg

salt and white pepper

1 slice of onion

1 bay leaf

SAUCE MORNAY:

1 cup of thin Béchamel

1/2 cup Parmesan or Gruyère cheese, grated

Mix ingredients for the batter, adding enough milk to give it the consistency of thin cream. Heat clarified butter in a heavy omelet pan over high heat. Pour a ladle-full of batter into the pan and tilt the pan so only a very thin film covers the bottom. Do not add too much batter or the crêpes will be too thick. When one side is cooked and lightly brown, flip the crêpe over and cook on the other side. As each crêpe is cooked, remove it from the pan and set aside in a warm place. You may like to stack them between sheets of greased paper. Cook the rest of the crêpes, adding additional clarified butter as needed.

Make the Béchamel sauce by melting the butter in a pan and whisking in the flour to make a roux. Bring milk to a boil with the nutmeg, onion slice, and bay leaf. Add this carefully to the roux, a little at a time, stirring so the sauce does not become lumpy. Bring to a boil, stirring all the while, then remove from the heat and stir in the grated cheese to make Mornay sauce. Season to taste, set aside, and keep warm.

Mix together the lobster, shrimp, and crabmeat and sauté briefly in clarified butter. Stir in half the Mornay sauce.

To assemble, place one crêpe on a serving plate. Place a spoonful or two of seafood mixture down the center of the crêpe and roll up. Place in an individual casserole dish and top with more Mornay sauce. Repeat with all six crêpes. You may prepare one large crêpe for each serving or two smaller ones. Place the casserole dishes under a broiler for a few minutes to brown the tops, and serve.

Seafood Spring Rolls with Orange Tamari Sauce

This delicacy comes from Christian's Restaurant in Chatham.

SERVES 6 TO 8 AS AN APPETIZER

3/4 cup shrimp, diced small

1/4 cup scallops, diced small

1/2 cup cooked lobster meat, diced small

1 bunch scallions, thinly sliced, whites only

1 tablespoon finely chopped garlic

1/2 cup shredded carrots

1/2 cup thinly sliced red peppers in 1" lengths

1 stalk celery, shredded

1½ cups shredded Savoy cabbage

2 tablespoon fresh grated ginger, or to taste

2 tablespoons soy sauce, or to taste

2 packages egg roll wrappers

sesame oil

ORANGE TAMARI SAUCE:

1 tablespoon sesame oil

1 scallion, thinly sliced

1 small clove garlic, finely chopped

1 cup orange juice

1 cup dark soy sauce

1 cup light stock (fish or chicken)

1/2 cup brown sugar

2 oz sake or dry white wine

2 tablespoons rice wine vinegar

  juice from one lime

1 or 2 teaspoons crushed red pepper, to taste

1 teaspoon grated fresh ginger

To make the sauce, pour sesame oil into a one quart saucepan and place over low heat. Add the sliced scallion and chopped garlic and sauté briefly. Add the remaining ingredients, and bring the entire mixture to a simmer. Adjust seasonings and add more soy sauce if desired. Remove from heat and leave to cool. This sauce can be served warm or cold.

Sauté the garlic and scallions quickly in sesame oil, then add the carrots and stir for a few minutes, then add the peppers, then the celery, and then the cabbage. Stir together and season with fresh grated ginger and soy sauce. Once mixture is heated through, remove from heat.

Sauté the diced shrimp and scallops very quickly in sesame oil, seasoning them with grated ginger and soy sauce. Do not overcook: this process should only take two minutes at the most. Add the cooked lobster meat and precooked vegetables and toss together to combine flavors. Cool in refrigerator.

When mixture has cooled, fill egg roll wrappers with seafood mixture, following the directions on the packet for folding. When all the egg rolls are wrapped, refrigerate them until ready to cook.

To cook the egg rolls, barely cover the bottom of a sauté pan with oil, preferably sesame oil. Set the flame to medium-high so the oil is hot enough that the egg rolls "talk" when they are cooked. Slowly turn the rolls in the pan until they are evenly browned. Serve with orange tamari dipping sauce as an appetizer.

Shellfish Algarve

This recipe is a specialty of Tim McNulty, chef of the popular Lobster Pot Restaurant in Provincetown. These ingredients serve one person; simply multiply ingredients for larger quantities.

SERVES 1

> **6 mussels, scrubbed**
>
> **4 quahogs, scrubbed**
>
> **2 oysters, scrubbed**
>
> **2 large shrimp, peeled**
>
> **2 oz scallops**
>
> **3 oz firm white fish, preferably cod or haddock**
>
> **6 oz olive oil**
>
> **2 oz clarified butter**
>
> **1 oz fish stock**
>
> **1 tablespoon minced garlic**
>
> **1 bay leaf**
>
> **pinch crushed red pepper**
>
> **6 oz rice noodles, cooked and cooled**

Heat the oil and butter in a gallon pot and add the fish stock and seasonings. Add the mussels, clams, and oysters to the pot, cover tightly, and simmer over medium-high heat until the shellfish begin to open. Shake the pot often. Add the shrimp, scallops, and fish and gently stir in. Let them just cook through, about 3 or 4 minutes. Do not overcook.

To serve, line a generous-sized pasta bowl with cooked rice noodles and arrange the shellfish on the noodles. Pour plenty of sauce on top. Garnish with chopped parsley and serve immediately. A feast for one!

For variation, you may like to add diced tomatoes to the sauce, or, for a really dramatic dish, top with a steamed lobster.

Seafood Saffron

This is another of Tim McNulty's signature dishes as served at the Lobster Pot Restaurant.

SERVES 1

2 medium shrimp, shelled

2 oz scallops

2 oz crabmeat (Snow or Dungeness)

2 oz clarified butter

4 oz spinach linguine

SAFFRON SAUCE:

1/2 pint dry white wine

1 oz minced shallots

tiny pinch of saffron threads

1 pint heavy cream

1 teaspoon Dijon mustard

salt and pepper to taste

To make the sauce, reduce the white wine in a heavy pot with the minced shallots and saffron until the pot is almost dry. Stir in the heavy cream, mustard, and seasonings and bring to a boil. Reduce by a quarter. You may add a little flour if the sauce needs thickening.

Meanwhile, cook the linguine al dente. Sauté the seafood in clarified butter for about 3 or 4 minutes. Drain the pasta when cooked and toss well with about one cup of the sauce. To serve, place linguine in a pasta dish, arrange seafood on top, and spoon more sauce over the seafood.

Insalata di Frutti di Mare

SEAFOOD SALAD

Truro artist and gourmet cook Judith Shahn gave me this recipe for her seafood salad, which is a feast in itself. Any combination of firm-fleshed fish and shellfish can be used for this dish.

SERVES 10 OR 12 AS A FIRST COURSE, OR FEWER PEOPLE AS A MAIN DISH

The proportions of any of the ingredients can be varied to taste.

3 dozen mussels

1 lb scallops

1 lb medium shrimp

1 lb squid

1 lb monkfish or other firm-fleshed fish

3/4 cup lemon or lime juice

1 cup dry white wine

1 red onion

1 garlic clove, minced

1 yellow onion, chopped

1 sweet red pepper

1 sweet green pepper

3 stalks celery

DRESSING:

3 garlic cloves, crushed

1 teaspoon coarse (kosher) salt

1/4 cup lemon juice

1/2 cup sherry vinegar

1 cup extra virgin olive oil

1 tablespoon fresh herbs, such as basil, dill, summer savory, thyme, or chervil, minced

To make the dressing, crush 3 garlic cloves to a paste with coarse salt. In a tightly lidded jar, mix the garlic with 1/4 cup of lemon juice, 1/2 cup of sherry vinegar, and one cup of olive oil. Add the herbs and shake the jar vigorously until its contents are well blended.

Rinse the scallops. Leave small bay scallops whole, but cut large sea scallops into halves or quarters. Macerate the scallops in a bowl in 3/4 cup lemon or lime juice and refrigerate for an hour or more, tossing a couple of times, until the scallops become opaque.

De-beard and scrub the mussels. Place them in a large pot with a tight-fitting lid with one minced garlic clove, the chopped yellow onion, and one cup of white wine. Steam until they open. Drain and save the broth. Remove the mussels from their shells, discarding any unopened ones. Mix with the dressing in a large bowl. Cover and refrigerate.

Shell and de-vein the shrimp. Bring the mussel broth to a full boil and drop the shrimp in, stirring to make sure all the shrimp make contact with boiling broth. Cook for a minute or so, just until the shrimp are pink and opaque. Drain the shrimp, once again saving every drop of the broth. Mix the shrimp with the mussels in the dressing and refrigerate.

Clean the squid thoroughly. Cut off the tentacles and slice them into 1" lengths. Slice the bodies into 1/4" rings. Bring the mussel liquor to a boil again, adding more water if necessary. Drop in the squid pieces and leave them in only until the liquid returns to a boil. Drain the squid thoroughly, mix with other seafood, and refrigerate.

Cut the monkfish, or other white fish, into pieces about 1" square. Bring the mussel broth to a boil again, adding more water if necessary. Cook the monkfish in boiling broth very briefly, only until the fish is opaque. Drain the fish, toss it lightly with the other cooked ingredients, and refrigerate. (Save the broth for another dish—it can form the stock for a wonderful soup or chowder, and will keep in the freezer.)

Cut the red onion, sweet green pepper, and sweet red pepper into thin strips. Dice the celery stalks. Mix the vegetables with the seafood mixture. Drain the scallops and toss them with the rest of the seafood mixture. Refrigerate the seafood salad for several hours or overnight, tossing occasionally. Taste to see if more salt is needed (it probably won't be), and add more if so desired.

This salad can be served on top of or accompanied by a tossed green leafy salad, with Portuguese or French bread, or garlic bread.

Unloading a fine catch of mackerel, c. 1915.

Photo: George Elmer Browne

Ground Fish

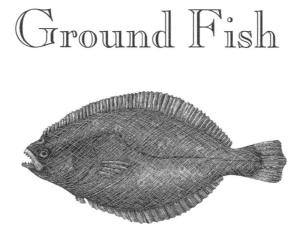

E veryone is familiar with the ground, or bottom fish, those white-fleshed fish that inhabit the lower regions of our coastal waters. Included in this category are cod, haddock, and flounder, and also lesser known species such as pollock, whiting, cusk, hake, and ocean perch. Most are caught in nets towed by draggers, though occasionally fish hooked by longline fishermen is found in local markets. This fish— sometimes known as Chatham cod, named for the town which harbors the largest longline fleet in the region—is the freshest fish available. In the spring, fish caught by Chatham trap fishermen in weirs—nets attached to poles driven into the sandy ocean bottom—is also available locally and is well worth seeking out for its high quality.

When Bartholomew Gosnold explored Cape Cod in the early 1600s he was amazed at the teeming shoals of fish in the surrounding waters and described Provincetown Harbor in his journal: "It is a harbour wherein one may anchor a thousand ships, and there we tooke great stoare of codfysshes . . ." and called the land Cape Cod. Those teeming shoals of the past have declined drastically due to ineffective federal management, but recent changes to catch limits and net size reduction seem to be bringing the stocks back.

Cod, both domestic and flash-frozen imported, is readily available in local fish markets, and haddock, which has suffered a severe decline in recent years, is making a comeback. Haddock is a versatile fish with a firm, fine texture and delicate unfishy flavor, and much in demand. Flounder is still plentiful, though expensive, due to the filleting process which wastes up to two-thirds of the fish. This family of flatfish includes yellowtail and black-back flounder as well as dabs and fluke. Sole is essentially a restaurant name for flounder. Grey sole, which can grow to 30" in length, has the best reputation with chefs due to its fine flavor and texture.

Scrod, which is a younger cod, or occasionally haddock, is a specialty of the New England region, traditionally served simply broiled with a knob of butter and a squeeze of lemon juice. At one time, scrod was evidently the name for a cheaper grade of fish—Molly Benjamin, a commercial fisherman, tells a fine tale about how scrod got its name: in the old days when the fishing boats went out to Georges Bank for days at a time and returned with their holds loaded up with salted cod, the boat captains would sell the top third of their catch for the highest prices; the middle third at lower prices; and the bottom layer, or "squished cod," at the lowest prices . . . hence the contraction "scrod."

All these species of fish lend themselves to a wide range of cooking methods: they can be boiled, poached, steamed, baked, smoked, broiled, and sautéed, though cod is the fish best suited for deep-frying. The most crucial thing about cooking fish is learning to recognise when it is done. Fish cooks very quickly and at a lower temperature than most meat, and the softer the flesh, the more quickly it will cook. Fish should be cooked *à point*, or just cooked, so it will fall apart easily when pressed gently with a fork. The flakes should be moist and succulent, the flesh soft, and warm rather than hot. The color will change from white to opaque and creamy white beads of curd will appear on the surface in the spaces between the flakes of fish. Fish that is cooked *à point* produces creamy curds and releases no juices. Fish that is fully cooked but still moist and good to eat has creamy curds and releases a small amount of juice, while overcooked fish has a pool of juice and will be hard and dry to the taste.

Cape Cod Fish Chowder

SERVES 4–6

1¹/₂ lbs haddock, cod or hake, cut into
  small pieces
1/2 lb salt pork or bacon fat, diced
1 large onion, chopped
2 potatoes, diced
2 bay leaves
2 cups water, more if needed
2 tablespoons flour
1 cup milk
1 cup light cream
2 oz butter
paprika

In a large pot, sauté the chopped onion in salt pork or bacon fat until lightly colored. Remove salt pork or bacon from the pot with a slotted spoon. Add the fish, diced potatoes, and bay leaves to the pot and cover with water. Simmer gently until the potatoes are cooked, about 30 minutes.

Mix the flour with the milk, stirring well so there are no lumps (or shake in a bottle until smooth.) Carefully add this mixture to the soup, stirring slowly. Simmer gently for about 5 minutes or until the flour has cooked. Add the cream and heat through, but do not boil.

Stir in the butter, sprinkle with paprika, and let the soup stand for a few minutes before serving. This chowder tastes even better the next day.

Broiled Haddock

SERVES 4

1 lb fresh haddock (or cod, halibut or flounder)
2 oz butter
1 cup breadcrumbs
juice of 1 lemon
salt and pepper to taste
fresh chopped parsley
paprika

Place fish, preferably filleted, in a baking pan lined with aluminum foil. Cut butter into pieces and place on top of the fish. Season with salt and pepper and sprinkle with breadcrumbs. Broil until lightly colored, about 10 minutes. Sprinkle lemon juice over the fish and broil for a few more minutes. Serve hot, garnished with fresh parsley and sprinkled with paprika.

Baked Cod or Haddock

*Preheat
oven to
350
degrees.*

1 whole haddock or cod fish, about 3 lbs,
   cleaned and de-scaled
2 tablespoons olive oil
1/2 lb salt pork, or 4 slices of bacon,
   cut into slivers
1 large onion, sliced
4 potatoes, peeled and quartered
1/2 cup milk
salt and pepper to taste
paprika
2 bay leaves
2 tablespoons flour

Rinse the fish in cold water and pat dry. You may leave the head on if you wish. Place the fish in a large baking pan and rub with olive oil. Cut slits on the surface of the fish with a sharp knife and place slivers of salt pork or bacon in the slits. Scatter onion slices over the fish and arrange the potatoes in the pan around it. Pour on the milk and sprinkle with salt, pepper, paprika, and bay leaves.

Sprinkle two tablespoons of flour over the fish and place the pan in the oven. Bake at 350 degrees for about 1½ hours, or until done, basting frequently with milk so the fish does not dry out.

This dish may be varied by adding chopped tomatoes and green pepper to the onions scattered over the fish, or fill the cavity of the fish with your favorite stuffing, mixed with a few chopped clams, scallops or shrimp.

Fried Fish Cheeks & Tongues

CARAS E LINGUAS DE PEIXE

An old-time classic from TRADITIONAL PORTUGUESE RECIPES FROM PROVINCETOWN *by Mary Alice Luiz Cook*

SERVES 4

1 lb cod or haddock cheeks and tongues
2 eggs, beaten in one cup of water
flour, seasoned with salt, pepper and paprika
vegetable oil for frying

Place seasoned flour in a paper or plastic bay. Dip fish into egg mixture, then into bag of flour. Fry in hot oil and drain on paper towels. This method of cooking fish is also perfect for swordfish, cut into small pieces.

Cheeks and tongues also make a delicious and inexpensive fish chowder.

Scrod Baked in Puff Pastry

SERVES 6 - 8

Preheat oven to 375 degrees.

3 lbs fresh scrod, cut in large steaks or fillets

2 lbs spinach

4 or 5 shallots, chopped

salt and pepper to taste

dash of nutmeg

2 lbs mushrooms, sliced

2 or 3 oz butter

1 sheet of puff pastry

1 egg

1/2 cup milk

Rinse the scrod and pat dry. Pick over the spinach and wash thoroughly. Steam the spinach lightly. Let cool and drain off excess water. Set aside. Chop the shallots and sauté in a skillet in butter. Season with salt and pepper and a dash of nutmeg. Add sliced mushrooms to the shallots and sauté for a few minutes until soft, adding more butter if needed. Set side.

Roll out the puff pastry into a large square. Spread the spinach mixture thinly across the pastry dough, covering it completely. Then spread the sautéed mushroom mixture on top of the spinach layer. Place the fish steaks on the mushroom layer in the center of the pastry and carefully wrap the dough around the fish. Mix the egg with the milk to make an egg wash and seal the pastry by wetting the edges. Paint the dough with egg wash to give it a good color while baking. Bake the scrod in the oven at 375 degrees until golden brown, about 20 or 30 minutes, depending on the thickness of the fish.

To serve, cut the pastry in slices about 1/2" thick and place portions on their side to show a center of white fish surrounded by a ring of mushrooms, a ring of spinach, and a layer of pastry.

Cape Cod Fish Cakes

SERVES 4 TO 6 | **1½ lbs haddock, cod or hake, cut into steaks**
2 large potatoes, peeled and quartered
2 eggs, slightly beaten
1 large onion, finely diced
1/4 cup fresh chopped parsley
salt and pepper to taste
1 tablespoon flour
1/2 cup olive oil, more if needed

Boil the fish and potatoes together in a saucepan for about 20 minutes. Bone and flake the fish when it is cooked and mash the potatoes.

Mix the flaked fish and mashed potatoes thoroughly and add the beaten eggs. Mix well.

Add the diced onion, chopped parsley, and seasonings to the fish mixture and mix well.

Form the mixture into balls, flatten them and dust with flour. Fry in hot olive oil until lightly browned on both sides. Drain on paper towels.

Fish cakes are traditionally served with baked beans. Fish cakes of a smaller size make an excellent party treat—serve them cold, with tartar sauce as an accompaniment, and spear with a toothpick.

Spicy Fish Cakes

SERVES 6

Preheat oven
to 325
degrees.

2 lbs cod or scrod, cut into steaks

2 cloves garlic, diced

3 shallots, diced

1/4 cup brandy

sprinkle of cumin, cayenne pepper and nutmeg

salt and pepper to taste

1/4 cup crème fraiche (see recipe on page 219)

2 tablespoons Dijon mustard

2 tablespoons chopped cilantro

2 tablespoons herbed breadcrumbs

1/2 cup olive oil

SAUCE:

1 cup fish stock

1 tablespoon crème fraiche

1 tablespoon chopped cilantro

1 tablespoon lemon juice

Place the garlic, shallots, and brandy in a roasting pan and lay the fish steaks over them. Season lightly with salt, pepper, cumin, cayenne, and nutmeg. Cover pan and bake for 40 minutes at 325 degrees. When the fish is baked, pour the juice from the pan into a container and save for the sauce. In a mixing bowl, break up the fish and mix well with the crème fraiche, mustard, cilantro, and breadcrumbs. Chill for an hour, then shape the mixture into cakes and sauté in olive oil until crisp.

Make the sauce by mixing a cup of fish stock with a little chopped cilantro, lemon juice, and crème fraiche. To serve, spoon a puddle of sauce on each serving plate and place two fish cakes on top.

Haddock Russe

A simple and delicious recipe from the menu of The Flagship in Provincetown when it was owned by Ciro Cozzi back in the 1970s.

SERVES 4

2 haddock fillets, about 2 lbs total

3 oz butter

1 small onion, chopped

1 cup white wine

1 cup water

1 bay leaf

1 tablespoon chopped parsley

pinch of dried tarragon

1 tablespoon tomato paste

1 cup sour cream

1 small cucumber, sliced and blanched

Melt an ounce of butter in a medium-sized skillet and add the chopped onions. Sauté until soft. Place the fish fillets in the skillet and cover with wine and water. Add the chopped parsley, bay leaf, and tarragon. Simmer (do not boil) until the fish is just cooked and still tender to the touch. Remove fillets carefully and keep warm. Strain the cooking liquid.

In a clean skillet, melt 2 oz of butter and blend in the tomato paste. Add half of the strained cooking liquid and reduce by one half. Turn down the heat and stir in the sour cream. Continue stirring until the cream mixture starts to bubble. To serve, arrange fish fillets on a platter and spoon the sauce over them. Garnish with blanched cucumber slices.

Haddock Baked with Dill Havarti

SERVES 4

Preheat oven to 350 degrees.

1¹/₄ lb haddock fillet

1 cup olive oil

1 tablespoon Worcestershire sauce

1 teaspoon snipped chives

salt and pepper to taste

1 cup white breadcrumbs

1/2 lb dill Havarti cheese

Mix olive oil, Worcestershire sauce, chives, salt and pepper together. Dip fish into the mixture, remove and shake off excess oil, and dip the fillets into breadcrumbs seasoned with salt and pepper. Place on a buttered baking sheet and bake for 20 minutes at 350 degrees. Just before the fish is done, top with sliced cheese (enough to cover the fish), and return the pan to the oven so the cheese melts completely over the fish. Serve immediately after the cheese has melted.

Creole Haddock or Cod

SERVES 4

1 lb haddock or cod

1/2 cup fish or chicken stock

2 tablespoons chopped celery tops

1 medium onion, chopped

1 clove garlic, chopped

2 tablespoons lemon juice

2 tablespoons dry white wine

1 teaspoon dried rosemary, crushed

1/2 teaspoon dried dill

1/2 teaspoon salt

1 green pepper, deseeded, cut into wedges

1 tomato, trimmed, cut into wedges

Heat the stock, celery tops, onion, and garlic in a medium-sized skillet for 10 minutes. Most of the liquid will evaporate.

Cut the fish crosswise into four even blocks. Place the fish skin-side up in the broth in the skillet. Pour lemon juice and wine over the fish and sprinkle with rosemary, dill, and salt. Add the pepper wedges and cook, uncovered, for 10 minutes. Turn the fish pieces over and add the tomato wedges to the skillet. Cover the skillet and cook gently for another 5 minutes, or until the fish flakes easily when tested with a fork. Serve with rice.

Poached Haddock with Mussels

SERVES 6

2 lbs haddock (or cod) cut into 6 steaks
4 dozen mussels
1/2 cup each julienned celery, carrots & zucchini
1 cup dry white wine
1/2 cup leeks or scallions, finely sliced
1/2 cup heavy cream
4 oz butter
1/4 teaspoon nutmeg
2 tablespoons fresh chopped parsley
salt and pepper to taste

Cover julienne vegetables with water in a pot and cook until tender but still firm. Strain the vegetables and reserve the cooking water to poach the fish. Clean and dry the fish. Scrub and de-beard the mussels. Place the mussels in a covered pot with a cup of water, a cup of white wine and the chopped leeks or scallions. Cover the pot and steam for 5 minutes or until the shells open. Discard any which do not open. Remove almost all of the mussels from their shells, saving a few in their shells for garnish. Combine the vegetable cooking water and the mussel broth and strain into a large skillet. Place the fish in the broth, cover, and gently simmer for 8 or 10 minutes until the fish is flaky. Transfer the fish to an ovenproof casserole and keep warm.

Reduce liquid quickly to half a cup. Stir in the cream and season with nutmeg, salt and pepper. Add the butter in small pieces, whisking the sauce constantly. Add the mussels and parsley and heat through. Pour sauce over the fish. To serve, top with a julienne of carrots, celery, and zucchini, and garnish with a few mussels in their shells.

Howard Mitcham's Haddock Amandine Meunière

Howard Mitcham was introduced to this recipe, a very old French classic, in New Orleans where it was traditionally prepared with speckled sea trout. He brought the recipe to Provincetown where he substituted native haddock, to great acclaim, and so began his career as a celebrated chef and cookbook author.

SERVES 6

6 haddock fillets, weighing 3/4 lb each
1 cup milk
1 cup flour
1/2 lb butter
juice of 2 lemons
1/4 lb sliced almonds
4 fresh mushrooms, sliced thinly

Rinse the haddock fillets and pat them dry. Dip them in milk, then dredge in flour, and shake off the excess. Melt the butter in a large skillet and place the fish in it, skin-side up; cook slowly until brown, then flip over with a spatula and brown the other side. Remember, this is a slow cook, not a hot fry, which would destroy the delicate flavor of the dish.

Remove the fish and place on warm serving plates. Add the lemon juice to the butter in the pan, followed by the almonds and sliced mushrooms. Raise the heat high and stir and scrape the bottom and sides of the pan to release any browned crumbs—these are delicious. Stir until the almonds turn a light golden brown (don't let them get too brown or they will taste bitter). Pour this sauce over the fish and serve immediately, piping hot.

Brandade de Morue

CREAMED SALT COD

This salt cod dish—a cross between a hash, a pâté, and a mousse—originated in Provence in the South of France, and is redolent with garlic and olive oil. It's a perfect example of the whole being greater than the sum of its parts—it is truly special, and easily made in a food processor, although you can use a mortar and pestle if you prefer to prepare it in the traditional way.

SERVES 6
AS AN
APPETIZER

1½ lbs salt cod, soaked for 24 hours in
    three changes of water
1 cup extra virgin olive oil
4 garlic cloves, chopped
a few dashes of Tabasco
dash of ground nutmeg
freshly-ground black pepper
1 cup heavy cream
juice of 1 lemon
1 cup mashed potatoes

Cut up the fish and place in a saucepan. Cover with cold water and bring to a boil. Lower the heat and boil gently for one and a half hours. Drain the fish, remove the skin and bones, and flake into small pieces. Set aside.

Place the olive oil and garlic in a blender or food processor and mix well. Add the flaked salt cod and cream it with the oil and garlic. Add the Tabasco, nutmeg, and black pepper to taste. Blend in the cream. Add a little lemon juice, blend and taste. Turn the hash into a mixing bowl and mix in by hand enough mashed potatoes to thicken it to your individual taste. Adjust seasonings, adding more lemon juice if desired.

To serve hot, heat the brandade in the oven for 10 minutes and serve with croutons brushed with olive oil and toasted in the oven. Served cold, it makes a good hors d'oeuvres at a cocktail party.

Cassoulet of Salt Cod

Salt cod was once the economic backbone of the local fishing industry, considered cheap fare in this part of the world, but now it's hard to come by. It can be pricey, but when soaked it doubles in bulk so a little goes further than you might imagine. Ask for a piece from the center of the cod, where the flesh is thickest and juiciest. You can also buy prepackaged moist salt codfish readily in stores but it doesn't have quite the same exquisite flavor as the bone dry codfish.

SERVES 6

Preheat oven to 375 degrees

8 oz haricot beans, soaked overnight and
   drained

1 lb salt cod, soaked for 24 hours in
   three changes of water

4 oz salt pork, cut into small dice

1 onion, diced

1 large carrot, diced

1/2 cup olive oil

6 cloves garlic, crushed

1 lb tomatoes, skinned, de-seeded and sieved

1 tablespoon tomato paste

1 teaspoon sugar

1 bay leaf

2 sprigs thyme

pinch saffron threads

2 tablespoon chopped parsley

1 cup dry white wine

2 tablespoons fresh coriander

salt and pepper

2 oz dried breadcrumbs

Put the soaked beans into a large pan, cover with water and bring to a boil. Simmer for 40 to 60 minutes until tender. Drain and reserve the cooking water. Drain and rinse the salt cod. Remove and discard skin and bones. Cut or tear the flesh into pieces about 1" square.

Fry the salt pork, onion, and carrot in olive oil until they begin to brown. Turn down the heat and add the garlic. Cook for a minute or so, then add the tomatoes, tomato paste, sugar, bay leaf, thyme, saffron, and half the chopped parsley. Cook over a moderate heat for 3 to 4 minutes, stirring occasionally. Now add one pint of the bean water, wine, haricot beans, and pepper—but no salt yet—and bring to a boil. Simmer, half covered, for 40 minutes. Crush a few beans against the side of the pan to thicken the sauce slightly. Add the salt cod and half the coriander and cook, barely simmering (boiling toughens salt cod) for 10 minutes. Adjust seasoning if necessary.

Transfer the mixture into a casserole dish. Mix breadcrumbs with the remaining parsley and coriander and spread evenly over the surface. Bake in an oven at 375 degrees for about 30 or 40 minutes until the crust is browned. Serve hot, with a crisp green salad.

Drying salt cod in Provincetown, c. 1890.
POSTCARD COURTESY OF NOEL W. BEYLE

Baked Flounder with Mushrooms

SERVES 4

Preheat oven to 350 degrees

2 lbs flounder fillets

1/2 teaspoon salt

1/2 teaspoon white pepper

1 tablespoon minced parsley

1/4 teaspoon ground thyme

1/2 cup dry vermouth or dry white wine

2 tablespoons lemon juice

4 oz butter

1 small onion, sliced

1/2 lb mushrooms, sliced

lemon wedges and parsley for garnish

Wash and dry the flounder fillets. Place them in a shallow buttered baking dish and sprinkle with herbs and seasonings. Pour over the vermouth and lemon juice. In a separate skillet, melt the butter and sauté the onion and mushroom slices until limp. Arrange the cooked onions and mushrooms over the fish and bake at 350 degrees for 15 to 20 minutes. Garnish with lemon and parsley.

Baked Fillet of Flounder

This is a simple, tried-and-true recipe which brings out the delicate flavor of fresh flounder. Do not use fillets that are too small—they tend to dry out while baking.

SERVES 4

Preheat oven to 350 degrees

4 large flounder fillets

4 oz butter

1 cup milk

1/4 cup breadcrumbs

salt and white pepper to taste

paprika

Butter a baking pan with half the butter. Wash the fillets and dry well. Place the fish fillets in the pan and top with the remaining butter. Pour the milk over the fish. Mix the breadcrumbs with the pepper and salt and sprinkle over the fish. Sprinkle with paprika and bake for about 20 minutes at 350 degrees.

Sole Turbans in Herbed Cream

SERVES 2

Preheat oven to 375 degrees.

1 lb grey sole or flounder fillets

2 tablespoons lemon juice

2 large eggs

1/2 cup heavy cream

dash of cayenne pepper

1 teaspoon fresh chopped basil

1 teaspoon fresh chopped chives

1 teaspoon fresh chopped tarragon

Rinse fish and pat dry. Roll each fish fillet up into a turban shape, starting with the narrow end, the darker side facing in. Arrange these "turbans" in a buttered baking dish and sprinkle with lemon juice. Beat the eggs and cream together and mix in cayenne pepper and the chopped herbs. Pour this mixture over the fish and cover the dish with foil. Place the dish in the oven and reduce heat immediately to 350 degrees. Bake for about 20 minutes, or until the sole flakes when prodded with a fork.

Sole Milanese

SERVES 2

1 lb fresh fillets of sole or flounder
1/2 cup flour
1 or 2 eggs, beaten
1/2 cup seasoned bread crumbs
1 Spanish onion, sliced
3 oz butter
pinch of salt and pepper
1 oz dry vermouth

Wash sole and dry thoroughly. Arrange three soup plates in a row and place flour in the first, beaten egg in the second, and seasoned bread crumbs in the third. Dip the sole fillets first into flour and shake off the excess. Dip the sole carefully into beaten eggs so each fillet is covered. Let excess drip off and then press each fillet into seasoned bread crumbs so the fillets are well coated. Shake off excess breadcrumbs. Heat 2 oz of butter in a pan and sauté the sole fillets on both sides until lightly browned. Remove from the pan and keep warm.

In a separate pan, sauté the sliced onions in 1 oz of butter for 3 or 4 minutes. Season to taste. Stir in the dry vermouth and cook over high heat for 30 seconds. Transfer the sautéed onions to a serving platter and place fish on top. Serve with rice and a green salad.

Fillet of Sole with Bananas & Pecans

This was one of the original dishes served by Howard Gruber and Edmond DiStasi at Front Street Restaurant in Provincetown when it first opened in 1975. As trail blazers, they loved experimenting with unusual combinations.

SERVES 4

Preheat oven to 375 degrees

2 lbs sole fillets

2 cups plain bread crumbs

1/2 cup melted sweet butter

4 bananas

4 oz butter

1/4 cup pecan halves

juice of 1 lemon, or more to taste

1 small wine glass of white wine

lemon wedges for garnish

Wash and dry the sole fillets. Dip each fillet in melted sweet butter and then in bread crumbs to coat completely. Place in a baking pan just large enough for the fish to fit in a single layer. Bake the sole for 10 minutes in the oven at 375 degrees. Meanwhile, slice the bananas into quarters lengthwise and then into halves. Lightly sauté the bananas in 4 oz butter. Remove the fish from the oven when cooked and arrange the sautéed bananas around the sole. Scatter the pecan halves on top and return the pan to the oven for 3 more minutes. Remove the pan from the oven and carefully transfer the fish, bananas and pecans to a heated serving platter.

Squeeze the juice of one lemon into the pan and add the white wine. Stir well, scraping up all the butter and pan juices to make a sauce. Pour over the fish and serve, garnished with lemon wedges.

Fillet of Sole Breaded with Walnuts

SERVES 6

3 lbs of sole or flounder fillets

2 eggs

1/2 cup light cream

1 cup seasoned flour

1 cup bread crumbs

salt and pepper to taste

1 cup finely chopped walnuts

3 tablespoons unsalted butter

lemon wedges to garnish

Rinse the fish and pat dry. Beat the eggs in a soup plate and mix with the cream. Mix the bread crumbs with the chopped walnuts and place in a second soup plate. Place flour seasoned with salt and pepper in a third soup plate. Dip the fillets into flour, shaking off the excess. Dip the floured fillets into the egg mixture, making sure they are totally covered with beaten egg. Then dip the fillets into the bread crumbs mixed with the chopped walnuts. Cook in butter until both sides are browned. Be careful not to break the fillets when turning them—they are very delicate. Serve with lemon wedges.

Stuffed Sole Marceline

This was a signature dish at the Red Inn in Provincetown when Ted and Marceline Barker owned it back in the 1970s. Its rich sauce transforms an everyday dish into a gourmet treat.

SERVES 6

Preheat oven to 350 degrees

12 small fillets of sole or flounder

STUFFING:

1 cup shredded crabmeat or chopped scallops

1/2 cup melted butter

6 cups white bread crumbs

2 teaspoons poultry seasoning

2 tablespoons Parmesan cheese

1/2 cup white wine

2 teaspoons lemon juice

2 teaspoons Worcestershire sauce

MARCELINE SAUCE:

4 cups lobster stock, fish stock or clam juice

1 cup light cream

2 tablespoons cornstarch

1 cup fresh lobster meat

pinch of tarragon

To make the sauce, reduce the lobster stock or clam juice in a saucepan to two cups. Stir in a cup of light cream. Thin the cornstarch with a little water and add to the saucepan. Mix in well and bring to a boil. (Thin with a little stock if the mixture seems too thick.) Stir in pieces of lobster meat and a sprinkling of paprika to add color. Add tarragon to taste. Set aside and keep warm while preparing the fish. Mix the stuffing ingredients with enough melted butter to bind the mixture. Rinse the fish and pat dry. Place a few spoonfuls of stuffing in the middle of each fillet and roll up. Place two rolled-up fillets in each of 6 small baking dishes. Bake for 10 to 15 minutes at 350 degrees. Pour the warm sauce over the fillets and serve immediately, sprinkled with a little paprika.

Paupiettes of Sole

The "sole" used in this recipe is actually yellowtail flounder. Select fillets of a uniform size so that the fish will cook evenly. This particular cooking method for sole lends itself to a variety of sauces—the recipe here is for Chardonnay sauce.

SERVES 4	**2 lbs flounder fillets**
	1 cup spinach, steamed
	1/2 cup sliced mushrooms
Preheat the oven to 350 degrees	**1 oz butter**
	1/2 teaspoon lemon juice
	1/2 cup white Chardonnay
	1 small shallot, chopped
	3 tablespoons butter
	Tabasco and Worcestershire sauce to taste
	pinch of nutmeg
	salt and pepper

To make the spinach-mushroom duxelles, sauté the fresh steamed spinach and the sliced mushrooms in butter. Stir in a dash of Tabasco and Worcestershire sauce. Season with a pinch of nutmeg, salt and pepper, and a squeeze of lemon juice. Cool the mixture and chop it finely by hand or in a food processor.

Preheat the oven to 350 degrees. Wash the fish fillets and pat them dry. Lay out the pieces of fish and spread a few spoonfuls of the duxelles mixture on each. Roll them up into a turban shapes. Repeat for all the fish and arrange the fillets in a baking tin. Pour a thin layer of water into the pan and cover with tin foil. Bake for 7 to 10 minutes in a medium oven.

To make the Chardonnay sauce, simmer and reduce the wine and chopped shallot to a thin, translucent layer. Stir in three tablespoons of room-temperature butter and heat gently. Place a spoonful of Chardonnay sauce onto each serving plate, place the paupiettes on the sauce, top each with a drizzle of sauce, and serve.

Flounder Véronique

A variation of the classic French recipe, traditionally served with green grapes.

SERVES 4

2 lbs flounder fillets

1½ cups white wine

1 stalk celery with leaves

1 sprig parsley

3 peppercorns

1 teaspoon salt

8 large mushroom caps, sliced

3 tablespoons butter

2 tablespoons flour

3/4 cup heavy cream, warmed

1 cup sweet green seedless grapes, halved

salt and white pepper to taste

Pour the wine into a large skillet and add the celery, parsley, peppercorns and 1 teaspoon salt. Carefully poach the fish in the white wine for 10 minutes or until just done. Remove and drain the fish on paper towels, leaving the stock in the pan. Transfer the fish to an ovenproof dish and set aside in a warm place. Reduce the wine stock left in the pan by half.

In a separate pan, sauté the mushrooms in one tablespoon of butter until soft. In another saucepan, melt 2 tablespoons of butter and stir in the flour. Cook gently while stirring for 2 minutes. Gradually stir in the warmed cream and 1/4 cup of the reduced wine stock and bring to a boil, stirring all the while to avoid lumps. Remove the pan from the heat, add the grapes and mushrooms to the sauce, and season to taste with salt and pepper. Pour sauce over the fish and place under the broiler for just long enough to brown slightly. Serve, garnished with a few whole grapes.

Almond-Crusted Sole with Grapefruit & Champagne Sauce

An innovative recipe from Jake Jacobus of Mulligans Restaurant in Brewster.

SERVES 4

4 5-oz fillets of sole or flounder

1/2 cup crushed toasted almonds

1/4 cup bread crumbs

1 egg, lightly beaten

1/2 cup flour

1/4 cup olive oil

GRAPEFRUIT & CHAMPAGNE SAUCE:

1/4 cup champagne

1/2 teaspoon minced shallots

4 tablespoons sweet butter

1/4 cup minced scallion greens

1 pink grapefruit, peeled and sectioned, with any juice

Mix almonds and bread crumbs together. Place the beaten egg, flour, and almond-crumb mixture in 3 separate soup plates. Rinse the fish and pat dry. Dip the fillets first in flour, then in beaten egg, and then in almond-crumb mixture, until all the fish is breaded.

Heat the olive oil in a sauté pan and brown the fillets on each side. Remove from the pan and place the fish in a warm oven (200 degrees) while you make the sauce.

Deglaze the pan with champagne. Add shallots and reduce liquid by one third. Add any grapefruit juice to the pan. Slowly whisk in 4 table-spoons of sweet butter. Finally, add the grapefruit sections and scallion greens to the pan and stir just enough to warm through. To serve, arrange fish on a platter and spoon sauce over the top.

PHOTO: TONY CHIARAPPO

Anton Stetzko, Jr., on Nauset Beach, Orleans, November 3, 1981, with his world-record breaking (73 lbs) striped bass, caught in the surf on a 17# line.

Sport Fish

The sport fish, caught in the surface waters of Cape Cod Bay and the surrounding Atlantic, generally have a darker, oilier flesh and a stronger flavor than the ground fish. This group of fish includes bluefish, swordfish, tuna, striped bass, salmon, and mako shark. They can be eaten as steaks or fillets, and are best broiled or baked, yet there are other delicious ways of preparing some of these species, as the following recipes demonstrate.

Sport fish have a texture more like meat than the more common white-fleshed bottom fish, and are loaded with nutrients and essential fatty acids, important for a healthy diet. The bluefish is the most plentiful and least expensive of these, and also the most ferocious. Known as the bully of the sea, blues are found all over the world. They travel in large schools like pack wolves, preying on anything that falls in their path. Striped bass and other large fish know to avoid a school of predatory bluefish. Blues are usually caught with a rod and line and should be eaten the same day.

Striped bass has a lighter color and flavor than bluefish. They are often caught off ocean beaches by sport fishermen, waiting patiently all night on an incoming tide for the chance to land a prize-winning catch. In danger of precipitous declines just a decade ago, the striped bass has made a remarkable recovery, one of the most thrilling of American restoration programs.

Much of the bluefin tuna caught off the Cape is shipped directly to Japan where it can fetch enormous prices, but some finds its way into local fish markets. Fresh grilled tuna has become a popular item on the menus of many local restaurants. It has a strong, rich flavor, and local chef Howard Mitcham advises soaking the fish in salty water for a couple of hours to leach out the blood before grilling. Tuna fishing is carefully regulated and special permits are required.

Mako shark—the most flavorful of the edible shark species—is another fish that has grown enormously in popularity in recent years, to the point where they are also becoming scarce. Sharks grow slowly and so are especially vulnerable. Perhaps the success exhibited in the regulation of striped bass will have similar benefits for the mako shark.

The exotic looking swordfish is found in all of the world's oceans and can weigh up to a thousand pounds, though locally-caught fish usually weigh in at about 200 pounds. It's available fresh in warm months, frozen off-season. When buying swordfish, make sure the flesh is gleaming and bright and the whorls are tightly closed; browning and gaping signify that the fish is deteriorating. Overcooked swordfish can be dry, chewy, and flavorless, so pay attention to cooking times. It benefits greatly from soaking in a marinade for an hour or so before grilling or broiling. Swordfish is not as versatile as other gamefish species, but it's a flavorful, meaty fish, especially suited to grilling because it stays in one piece on the grill.

Wild Atlantic salmon was essentially extinct due to industrial pollution of New England rivers where it spawns, but restoration efforts are showing hopeful signs. The vast majority of salmon found in our local fish markets is farmed, though occasionally wild fish from Alaska may be available. Farmed salmon is rich and fatty—sometimes it actually looks marbled—and has the added advantage of being available year-round. With its pinkish orange flesh and sweet, rich flavor, salmon is a versatile fish that lends itself to a variety of cooking methods, and is also one of the few fin fish that tastes as delicious cold as hot.

Grilled Striped Bass

This basic recipe for cooking bass is perfect for grilling the fish right at the beach. Striped bass is one of the few species of local fish that is firm enough to grill without falling apart—tuna and swordfish are also suitable for this method of cooking.

SERVES 4

1¹/₂ lb fillet of striped bass, about 1" thick

2 tablespoons olive oil

1 clove garlic, minced (optional)

salt and freshly ground black pepper

lemon wedges

Start a charcoal or wood fire: it should be very hot, and the grate clean. Wipe the fish dry and drizzle with olive oil. Sprinkle it with the minced garlic, salt and pepper. When the coals are white, grill the fish, flesh-side down first, for about 5 minutes, inserting a metal spatula between the fish and the grill every 2 minutes or so to prevent sticking. Turn the fish over and grill for another 5 minutes, again making sure the fish doesn't stick. When cooked, the fish should be opaque but still juicy. To make sure, you can lift the flesh up with a fork and peek inside (seasoned cooks use the finger test—press for firmness, the flesh should be neither too firm nor too soft.) Serve immediately, skin-side down, with lemon wedges. A delicious marinade, which also serves as a sauce, can be made with the following ingredients:

1/4 cup soy sauce

2 cloves garlic, crushed

1/4 cup olive oil

1 tablespoon fresh ginger, finely chopped

1 tablespoon grated orange peel

1/4 cup sherry or Madeira

Mix all ingredients for the marinade in a shallow bowl and marinate the fish in this mixture for at least an hour before grilling, turning several times. Grill the fish as above, basting with the marinade.

Baked Portuguese Striped Bass

This is one of my favorite ways to prepare fish—it's speedy, simple, and delicious, and even children like it! It also works well with other kinds of fish, particularly bluefish and cod.

SERVES 6

Preheat oven to 375 degrees

6 striped bass steaks,
4 oz salt pork
1 large onion, sliced
1 green pepper, sliced
3 tomatoes, sliced in rounds
1/4 teaspoon cumin
salt and freshly ground black pepper
1 cup white wine
Parmesan cheese

Fry out the salt pork until brown, and set aside. Lay the bass steaks, skin side down, on greased aluminum foil in a large baking pan. Layer the onions, green pepper, and tomatoes over the fish in that order. Sprinkle the cumin and seasonings on top of the fish. Pour the white wine into the pan and add the diced salt pork. Bake the fish for 15 minutes; remove the pan from the oven and sprinkle the fish with Parmesan cheese. Return to the oven and bake for 5 more minutes or until the cheese is brown.

Striped Bass au Gratin

SERVES 4

4 striped bass steaks or fillets
1 cup dry white wine
3 cups water
1 small onion, coarsely chopped
1 stalk celery, coarsely chopped
1 teaspoon salt
1 bay leaf
4 oz butter
4 oz flour
2 cups cream
8 oz mild Cheddar cheese, grated
1/4 cup dry sherry
salt and pepper
a pinch of cayenne pepper
1/2 cup white bread crumbs
chopped parsley

Mix 3 cups of water with a cup of white wine and add the onion, celery, bay leaf, and a teaspoon of salt. Pour into a shallow pan large enough to hold the fish and poach the bass gently for 20 minutes or until done. Remove fish from the stock and flake into a buttered casserole dish.

Melt the butter in a saucepan. Add the flour and stir until blended. Warm the cream and add to the roux a little at a time, stirring briskly so the sauce is smooth. Bring to a boil, stirring all the while, and add the grated cheese and sherry. Heat to boiling and season to taste. Mix the sauce with the flaked fish in the casserole dish. Sprinkle with bread crumbs and bake for 35 to 45 minutes at 350 degrees. Garnish with parsley.

Medallions of Striped Bass with Cider & Ginger Cream

This delicious recipe comes from the elegant Regatta restaurant in Cotuit.

SERVES 4 | 6 oz striped bass per person
3 oz butter
12 apple rings
6 shallots, minced
1 teaspoon diced fresh ginger
1 cup dry cider
1 cup heavy fish stock, warmed
1½ cups heavy cream
salt and white pepper to taste
1 bay leaf
pinch of ground thyme and nutmeg
1 teaspoon unsalted butter

Cut the fish into medallions about 1/4" thick. Rinse the fish and pat dry. Melt the butter in a skillet and dredge the fish in flour. Sauté the fish lightly on both sides in butter for a few minutes until just cooked through. Remove fish from pan and set aside in a warm place.

Add the apple slices to the pan and cook for just long enough to warm them through. Set aside. Add shallots and ginger to the pan and sauté lightly, adding more butter if necessary. Do not brown. De-glaze the pan with the cider and add seasonings. Stir in the hot fish stock, and then the cream, and reduce slowly by half, stirring all the while, being careful not to scorch the sauce. Adjust seasoning and whip in a teaspoon of un-salted butter. Strain the sauce.

To serve, arrange 3 medallions of bass on each warmed serving plate and place one apple ring on top of each piece of fish. Pour sauce over the fish and garnish with a sprig of fresh dill.

Poached Bass with Clams

This dish—"Pesce alla Giosue"—is a perennial favorite at Ciro & Sal's,
Provincetown's popular Italian restaurant.

SERVES 8

1 8-lb striped bass, cut into 1 lb steaks

16 littleneck clams, well scrubbed

1/4 cup olive oil

8 medium-sized shallots, chopped

1 clove garlic, minced

1/4 cup fresh chopped basil

salt and pepper

1/2 teaspoon dried thyme

2 cups dry white wine

1/4 cup chopped fresh chives

2 tablespoons chopped fresh parsley

Heat oil in a large skillet. Add the bass steaks and sauté lightly on both sides. Reduce heat and add the clams, chopped shallots, garlic, basil, thyme, salt and pepper. Pour in 2 cups of white wine and add enough water to cover. Poach gently, being careful not to boil the fish. When the clams open (about 10 minutes), add the chives and cook for another 2 or 3 minutes.

To serve, remove the bass steaks from the poaching liquid and place on serving plates. Arrange clams around the fish, spoon a little broth over the steaks and garnish with parsley.

Crispy Striped Bass with Garlic Sauce

SERVES 4

2 lb fillet of striped bass
1 large egg, beaten
flour for dredging
1/2 cup sesame oil
1½ tablespoons minced garlic
1 teaspoon peeled and minced fresh ginger
1 tablespoon sherry
1/2 cup fish or chicken stock
1 tablespoon soy sauce
1/4 teaspoon chili-garlic paste,
**   or hot sauce, to taste**

Rinse the fish and pat dry. Dredge in flour, dip into beaten egg, then back into flour. Heat a large non-stick skillet over a medium flame for 3 minutes. Pour in oil to cover the bottom to a depth of 1/8 of an inch. When the oil shimmers, toss a pinch of flour in—if it sizzles, the oil is hot enough. Place the fish carefully in the oil and raise the heat to high. Cook for about 4 minutes, watching vigilantly and adjusting the flame so the fish browns but does not burn. Turn it carefully and brown the other side for about 4 minutes. Test for doneness by piercing the fish with a knife blade—if it cuts the fish easily, it's done. Remove the pan from the heat and drain the fish on kitchen paper. Wipe the hot pan clean with kitchen paper and add a tablespoon of oil. Turn heat to high and sauté the garlic and ginger for half a minute. Add the sherry—it will cook away almost immediately. Add the stock and cook for 30 seconds or so. Add the soy sauce and cook for another few seconds. Add the chili-garlic paste and stir in well. Add a little stock if it seems too thick. Pour the sauce over the fish and serve immediately with fragrant Basmati rice.

Lincoln's Blackened Swordfish with Mango-Melon Chutney

A delicious, fruity swordfish recipe from Bill Conway, chef-owner of the Captain Linnell House in Orleans, a former sea captain's mansion.

SERVES 4

4 swordfish steaks, 6-8 oz each, about 1" thick

4 tablespoons prepared Cajun seasoning

1/2 cup olive oil

CHUTNEY:

1 ripe mango, peeled and diced small

2 cups diced canteloupe

1 cup diced red onion

1 cucumber, peeled, seeded and diced

1 cup chopped, seeded and diced tomato

1 tablespoon fresh chopped mint or basil

1 tablespoon chopped fresh parsley

juice from one lime

BEURRE BLANC:

1 cup white wine vinegar

1 tablespoon chopped shallots

1/2 lb butter, cut into pieces

Combine all ingredients for the chutney in a large bowl with 2 tablespoons of olive oil. Chill until ready to use. To make the beurre blanc, place shallots and vinegar in a small saucepan and bring to a boil. Reduce until almost dry. Lower heat and whisk in the butter, a little at a time, until it is all incorporated. The sauce should be light and creamy; keep it warm but not hot. Mix 1/2 cup olive oil with Cajun seasoning to make an oily paste. Coat swordfish steaks thoroughly with this and grill for 3-5 minutes on each side until done (the skin should peel away easily when cooked). To serve, place about 1/2 cup of chutney on each plate and top with a swordfish steak. Finish with a few spoonfuls of sauce.

Swordfish Baked in Foil

SERVES 4

*Preheat
oven to
425
degrees*

4 swordfish steaks

1 cup sliced mushrooms

1 medium onion, sliced

2 tablespoons finely chopped green pepper

   or chopped parsley

2 tablespoons lemon juice

2 tablespoons olive oil

1/2 teaspoon dill

salt and pepper to taste

4 small bay leaves

4 thick tomato slices

In a bowl, mix together the mushrooms, onion, pepper, lemon juice, olive oil, dill, salt and pepper. Line a baking dish with aluminum foil, spread half the vegetable mixture over the bottom, and place the swordfish steaks on top. Sprinkle with salt and pepper to taste. Place a bay leaf and a tomato slice on top of each steak and cover with the remaining vegetable mixture. Cover the pan with foil and bake at 425 degrees until the fish flakes easily, about 45 minutes. Serve the swordfish steaks topped with the vegetables and spoon sauce over the top.

Bayberry Swordfish Kebabs

This recipe, created by Betty Bodian, a painter who summers in Provincetown, is a variation of a Greek style of grilling swordfish which imparts a wonderfully delicate flavor. Bayberry, which is abundant on Cape Cod, has a taste similar to, but weaker than, the bay leaf.

SERVES 4

2 lbs swordfish, cut into 1" cubes

2 cups bayberry leaves without berries

1 large onion, coarsely chopped

4 garlic cloves, chopped

1 handful parsley, chopped

1/2 cup olive oil

1/2 cup red wine vinegar

salt and pepper

Wash the bayberry leaves and combine them in a shallow bowl with the onion, garlic, parsley, olive oil, and vinegar. Mix well and season with salt and pepper. Marinate the swordfish in this mixture for no more than 6 hours, turning the fish frequently to make sure it marinates evenly. Thread the cubes of swordfish on skewers with bits of bayberry leaves and onion clinging to them, and grill them over an even charcoal fire. The steaks may also be grilled on a grate covered by perforated foil.

Swordfish Diable

Named for the devil, this dish is hot and spicy!

SERVES 4

4 thin swordfish steaks, 6 oz each

1 tablespoon olive oil

salt and pepper to taste

1/4 lb sweet butter

1 teaspoon crushed hot red pepper flakes,
 or to taste

1 heaping teaspoon chopped scallions

1 tablespoon chopped shallots

1 tablespoon chopped parsley

juice from a good-sized lemon

Rinse the fish and pat dry. Heat the oil in a large frying pan. Season both sides of the swordfish steaks with salt and pepper. Sauté the fish in a very hot pan for 2 to 4 minutes on each side. Place each cooked swordfish steak on a heated dinner plate and keep warm. Pour the leftover oil out of the pan and add the sweet butter, hot red pepper flakes, scallions, shallots, parsley, and lemon juice. Cook for no more than a minute, scraping the pan and stirring all the while, making sure the butter does not burn. Spoon the sauce over the swordfish and serve immediately.

Swordfish Steaks with Peppercorn & Garlic Sauce

SERVES 4

4 swordfish steaks

2 tablespoons green peppercorns

6 tablespoons lemon juice

4 tablespoons olive oil

freshly ground sea salt

1 egg

1 clove garlic, roughly chopped

1/3 cup olive oil

1 teaspoon dried oregano

salt and freshly-ground black pepper

Lightly crush the green peppercorns using a pestle and mortar. Mix the lemon juice with 4 tablespoons of olive oil and salt to taste. Mix in the crushed peppercorns. Place the swordfish steaks in a shallow ovenproof dish and pour the peppercorn marinade over the steaks so that they are all well covered. Refrigerate overnight, turning once or twice.

Mix together the egg and garlic in a blender or food processor. With the machine still running, gradually pour in the olive oil a little at a time onto the egg and garlic mixture. As the olive oil is incorporated, you may increase it to a steady stream until it is all blended in and the sauce is thick. Don't rush this process.

Preheat the boiler and arrange the marinated swordfish steaks on the broiler rack. Sprinkle the oregano over the swordfish and season well with salt and freshly-ground black pepper. Broil for 15 minutes, turning the steaks frequently and basting with the marinade. When the steaks are cooked, transfer them to individual serving plates and top with some marinated peppercorns. Spoon over a generous portion of garlic sauce and serve.

Baked Portuguese Swordfish

SERVES 4

Preheat oven to 350 degrees

4 swordfish steaks, cut about 1/2" thick

1/2 cup olive oil

2 garlic cloves, minced

2 onions, sliced

bunch of scallions, chopped

salt and white pepper to taste

1 bay leaf

2 tablespoons capers

2 whole cloves

pinch of oregano

pinch of paprika

1 tablespoon lime or lemon juice

1 cup dry white wine

Pour the olive oil into a baking pan large enough to hold the swordfish steaks in a single layer. Scatter onion slices and minced garlic over the bottom of the pan; then add the scallions, bay leaf, capers, cloves, oregano, and paprika. Rub the steaks with lemon or lime juice and salt and pepper and place in the pan over the onions. Pour a cup of white wine over everything and bake in the oven at 350 degrees for 25 minutes or until the fish is tender and flakes easily with a fork. Baste the fish frequently while baking to keep it from drying out.

To serve, remove the whole cloves and arrange the swordfish steaks on a warmed platter. Cover with the onions and pan juices and garnish with parsley sprigs and lemon wedges.

Garlic Swordfish with Salsa Fresca

SERVES 4

Preheat oven to 500 degrees

4 swordfish steaks, about 8 oz each

1 clove garlic, cut into tiny slivers

2 tablespoons olive oil

salt and black pepper to taste

SALSA FRESCA:

1 clove garlic, crushed

1 jalapeño pepper, minced

1/4 cup chopped cilantro

2 cups chopped ripe tomatoes with their juice

1 small onion, finely chopped

1 teaspoon red wine vinegar

salt and freshly-ground black pepper to taste

Make small cuts into the flesh of the swordfish about 1 inch apart with a sharp knife point and push garlic slivers into the cuts. Pour a tablespoon of olive oil into a baking pan and lay the fish in the pan. Brush the top of the fish with the remaining oil and sprinkle with salt and pepper to taste. Heat the oven to 500 degrees and while the oven is warming up, make the salsa by mixing all the ingredients together in a bowl. Place the baking pan in the oven and cook the swordfish for 10 or 15 minutes until cooked. The fish is ready when the flesh flakes and is opaque. Serve immediately, with fresh salsa on the side.

Swordfish with Sesame & Cumin Crust

Another delectable recipe from the Regatta Restaurant of Cotuit.

SERVES 4

4 swordfish steaks
2 tablespoons sesame seeds
2 tablespoons cumin seeds
2 tablespoons coriander seeds
1/2 cup bread crumbs
juice and zest of 6 limes
2 pieces of fresh ginger, thumb-sized, diced
splash of ginger brandy
8 oz white wine
8 oz whole unsalted butter
dash of cream

Grind up a mixture of the sesame, cumin, and coriander seeds and mix with the bread crumbs.

Squeeze the limes and pour their juice into a saucepan with the ginger, wine, brandy, and half of the lime zest. Reduce over medium heat until the liquid has reduced to a syrup. Add a dash of cream and whisk in the butter, slowly adding small pieces one at a time. When all the butter has been added, season to taste and pour the sauce through a fine strainer into a container to keep it warm for a few minutes.

Lightly oil the swordfish steaks and press the seed mixture into the flesh, coating each side. Sauté over medium heat for 3 minutes or so on each side, depending on the thickness of the fish. When the sauce is ready, spoon a large puddle of the lime sauce onto warmed dinner plates and place a swordfish steak in the center of each plate. Garnish with a sprinkling of lime zest.

Smoked Bluefish Pâté

This bluefish pâté is a speciality of the Bramble Inn in Brewster and is served as part of a smoked seafood platter. The pâté is piped through a pastry bag fitted with a star tip and arranged on a platter with smoked salmon and smoked mussels, garnished with capers, chopped onion and toast points. You may add a heaping tablespoon of Dijon mustard or the grainy Moutard de Meaux to this mixture to add texture and spice.

SERVES 10

1 lb smoked bluefish

3/4 lb cream cheese at room temperature

2 tablespoons horseradish sauce

1 heaping tablespoon finely-chopped onion

1 tablespoon chopped fresh parsley

1/4 teaspoon cayenne pepper, or to taste

freshly-ground black pepper to taste

Pull the smoked bluefish apart into large flakes and pile them into a food processor fitted with a steel blade. Work the bluefish until it is all broken up. Blend in the cream cheese, horseradish sauce, onion, parsley, black pepper, and cayenne pepper to taste and continue working the mixture in on-off motions until it is smooth. Taste the mixture for seasoning and add more horseradish sauce, cayenne, or onion to suite your individual taste.

Pack the pâté into a decorative bowl and serve with unsalted crackers or homemade French bread toast points.

Grilled Bluefish with Rosemary

This recipe works well with other dark-fleshed fish such as mackerel and tuna, and also with swordfish and bass.

SERVES 4

2 bluefish fillets, about 2 lbs total

juice of 1 lemon

1/2 cup olive oil

1 small onion, minced

1 tablespoon crushed fresh rosemary

fresh rosemary sprigs

salt and freshly-ground black pepper

Rinse the fish and cut the fillets in half. Leave the skin on. Combine the lemon juice, olive oil, onion, rosemary, and seasonings. Pour this mixture over the fish and marinate for at least 30 minutes, turning occasionally.

While the fish is marinating, start a charcoal fire. When the fire has a good heat, toss a few sprigs of fresh rosemary directly onto the coals. Grill the fish over the coals, skin side up, for 4 or 5 minutes. Baste with the marinade and turn, grilling the fish on the other side for another 4 or 5 minutes. A fish basket makes this job easier; if you are not using one, run a spatula under the fish while it is grilling so it doesn't stick to the grate. The flesh will become white when cooked—use a paring knife to check that the fish is cooked at its thickest part.

Poached Bluefish

SERVES 4

4 bluefish steaks or fillets

1/2 cup sliced mushrooms

2 cups light cream

1 clove garlic, crushed

salt and white pepper to taste

1 tablespoon dry vermouth

Mix the cream, garlic, and vermouth and season with salt and pepper. Add the mushrooms and pour the mixture into a skillet large enough to hold the fish. Bring to a light boil, stirring to blend the flavors. Add the bluefish and poach gently for about 10 or 15 minutes. The fish is cooked when the flesh is white and opaque and a knife goes through with no resistance. To serve, place one fillet on each serving plate and top with a generous spoonful of sauce. Accompany with steamed rice.

Baked Bluefish Mediterranean

SERVES 4

*Preheat
oven to
350 degrees*

2 bluefish fillets, about 2 lbs

3 oz butter

2 tablespoons olive oil

1/2 lb mushrooms, sliced

1 small onion, thinly sliced

2 green peppers, deseeded and thinly sliced

1/4 cup chopped parsley

3/4 lb tomatoes, peeled and chopped

2 tablespoons lemon juice

1/4 cup vermouth

1/2 cup bread crumbs

Butter an ovenproof baking dish large enough to hold the fish in a single layer. In a skillet heat 2 oz butter with 2 tablespoons of olive oil. Sauté the mushrooms, onions, peppers, and parsley until the onions are limp and the mushrooms softened. Add the chopped tomatoes and continue cooking for a few more minutes. Place the fish in the buttered baking dish and rub with lemon juice. Pour vermouth over the fish and spread the vegetable mixture on top. Sprinkle with bread crumbs and dot with the remainder of the butter. Bake at 350 degrees for 25 minutes or until the bluefish flakes easily.

Hunan Bluefish

This tasty method of baking bluefish comes from the Impudent Oyster restaurant in Chatham.

SERVES 6

Preheat oven to 425 degrees

3 fresh bluefish fillets, about 3 lbs

1/4 cup garlic butter

2/3 cup soy sauce

1/3 cup dry sherry

1/2 cup sugar

4 large cloves garlic, diced

1 oz fresh ginger, grated

1½ cups freshly-squeezed orange juice

2 or 3 diced Hunan chilies

1 bunch scallions, slivered

Cut the bluefish fillets in half. Place the fish in a baking dish and dot with garlic butter. Mix soy sauce, sherry, sugar, garlic, and ginger in a small saucepan. Bring to a boil and remove from heat immediately. Add orange juice and chilies to the sauce. Pour sauce over the fish and scatter scallions on top. Bake for 20 or 25 minutes in the oven at 425 degrees. Serve with rice.

Baked Bluefish Stuffed with Wellfleet Oysters

This recipe illustrates perfectly the exuberance with which the late, great chef Howard Mitcham liked to prepare fish; from THE PROVINCETOWN SEAFOOD COOKBOOK.

SERVES **10**

Preheat oven to 350 degrees

1 whole bluefish, about 5 lbs

36 Wellfleet oysters, freshly shucked, retain the liquor

1 cup white wine

freshly-ground black pepper

3 or 4 slices of French bread

2 oz butter, melted

Clean and scale the fish and remove the head. Place the oysters and their liquor in a pan with a cup of white wine. Add a little black pepper. Poach the oysters gently until their edges curl; drain off the broth and use it to wet down and knead 3 or 4 slices of French bread into a paste. Mix this paste with the oysters and stuff the bluefish with it. Sew up the fish, lay it on greased aluminum foil in a baking pan, and bake at 350 degrees for 30 minutes, or until the fish is browned and cooked through. Brush it a couple of times with melted butter during the baking to keep it from drying out.

To serve, arrange the whole fish on a platter on a bed of lettuce leaves. Accompany with a freshly-made tomato sauce on the side and a bottle of chilled white wine.

Tuna Steak au Poivre

Fresh tuna has a texture similar to beef and adapts to this classic recipe perfectly, as served by Tim McNulty at the Lobster Pot Restaurant in Provincetown.

SERVES 4

Preheat oven to 300 degrees

4 tuna steaks, 6 to 8 oz each

4 teaspoons coarsely-ground black pepper

1/4 cup olive oil

1 tablespoon minced shallots

2 tablespoons green peppercorns

3/4 cup brandy

3/4 cup fish stock

1¹/₂ cups heavy cream

salt and pepper to taste

Season the tuna on both sides with coarsely-ground black pepper, pressing it into the flesh. Heat the oil in a skillet until just smoking. Brown the tuna steaks on both sides. Transfer them to a pan to finish in the oven at 300 degrees for about 7 minutes, depending on their thickness.

Remove some of the oil from the pan and sauté the shallots and green peppercorns in the remaining oil for a few minutes. Pour in the brandy and carefully flame off the alcohol. Reduce to half and add the fish stock. Reduce further to half a cup. Add the cream and reduce again until the mixture coats the back of the spoon. Season with salt and pepper; you can be heavy with the pepper. To serve, ladle some sauce on heated serving plates and place a peppered tuna steak on the sauce.

Grilled Tuna Steak with Tomato-Caper Chutney

Tim McNulty serves this spicy recipe at the Lobster Pot Restaurant in Provincetown.

SERVES 2

2 8-oz tuna steaks
daikon radish, shredded
MARINADE:
8 oz peanut oil
4 oz soy sauce
1/2 tablespoon honey
1/2 tablespoon Dijon mustard
4 oz puréed onion
1/2 tablespoon puréed ginger root
1/2 tablespoon puréed garlic
CHUTNEY:
1 large tomato, deseeded and chopped
4 oz cucumber, deseeded, peeled and diced
1 teaspoon capers, drained and rinsed
1 tablespoon thinly-sliced scallion
1/2 teaspoon puréed ginger root
1/2 teaspoon puréed garlic
pinch of freshly-ground black pepper

Place all ingredients for the marinade in a bowl and blend with a wire whisk, or mix in a food processor. This can be made up to 4 days ahead of time, and can also be used several times before being discarded.

Place all ingredients for the chutney in a sauté pan and cook slowly for about 15 minutes, mixing until well blended. This can be made up to 2 days ahead of time. Marinate the tuna for 10 minutes. Shake off the excess marinade and grill for 5 minutes on each side, depending on the thickness of the steaks. Serve with raw daikon radish and warm chutney.

Moroccan Grilled Tuna

Here is an exotic dish from the Captain Freeman Inn in Brewster which is equally delicious adapted to chicken or pork.

SERVES 2

2 freshly-cut tuna steaks, 1½" thick

8 dried apricots

3 tablespoons cognac or white wine

MARINADE:

1 tablespoon crushed garlic

2 tablespoons fresh lemon juice

1/2 teaspoon ground cinnamon

1/2 teaspoon cayenne pepper

1 teaspoon cracked black pepper

1 teaspoon salt

1 teaspoon cumin powder

1/4 cup olive oil

Light a charcoal fire. Mix the ingredients for the marinade, pour over tuna steaks, and massage into the flesh. Let the tuna marinate for an hour before grilling.

Pour the cognac or white wine over the apricots in a small glass bowl. Cover and microwave for one minute on high. Stir, and let sit for 20 minutes before serving.

Grill the tuna over hot coals for 4 to 5 minutes on each side until done, but do not overcook! Serve the tuna with apricots and couscous or rice with fresh snow peas.

Salmon en Croûte with Citrus Dill Beurre Blanc

SERVES 4

Preheat oven to 475 degrees

2 lb salmon fillet, cut into 4 equal pieces

12 sheets phyllo dough

1/2 lb melted butter, more if needed

1 lb arugula

1 cup sour cream

4 tablespoons fresh dill

3 tablespoons butter

fresh dill sprigs for garnish

CITRUS DILL BEURRE BLANC:

2 cups heavy cream

1/2 cup white wine

1/4 cup lemon juice

2 tablespoons butter, cut up into small pieces

1 tablespoon fresh chopped dill

Remove any bones from the salmon with a pair of needlenose pliers or tweezers. Mix 2 tablespoons of chopped fresh dill with the sour cream and set aside. Sauté the arugula in butter over medium heat until limp and set aside. Combine the cream, wine, and lemon juice in a saucepan and reduce by half, stirring constantly, until the mixture has thickened and coats the back of a spoon. Stir in the pieces of butter until the sauce is smooth. Add 2 tablespoons of chopped dill and set aside in a warm place.

Separate three sheets of phyllo dough, covering the remainder of the dough with a damp towel. Place one sheet of dough on a clean surface and brush the top with melted butter. Place a second sheet on top of the first and brush with butter; cover with a third sheet and brush with butter. This dough will make the crust. Repeat with the remaining dough. Place one quarter of the sautéed arugula on each piece of phyllo dough. Top with a portion of salmon, and then top that with a quarter of the sour cream blend. Fold the dough over to form packages and seal and trim edges as needed. Place the four packages of fish on a cookie sheet, brush with melted butter, and bake for 12 or 15 minutes or until golden brown.

To serve, spoon citrus dill beurre blanc to cover half of a dinner plate. Place a salmon en croûte in the center of each plate and garnish with fresh dill sprigs.

Copyright 1905 by the Rotograph Co.

A 6788   Lewis Bay and Harbor, Hyannis, Mass.

Lewis Bay, Hyannis Harbor, 1905, now known as Hyannisport,
where the ferry boats pick up passengers.

POSTCARD COURTESY NOEL W. BEYLE

Salmon Adriatico

1 salmon fillet, about 6 oz
1 oz butter
1 tablespoon olive oil
6 green olives, pitted and sliced
1 tablespoon capers
1 slice smoked salmon, cut into thin strips
1/2 wine glass dry vermouth
pinch saffron or turmeric
1/2 cup heavy cream
1 oz brandy
roasted red peppers for garnish

Sauté the salmon fillet in butter and olive oil over medium heat for about 4 or 5 minutes on both sides so it is almost cooked, but not quite. Remove the salmon and keep warm in the oven. Add the green olives, capers and smoked salmon to the pan and sauté for one minute. Add the dry vermouth, saffron or turmeric, heavy cream, and brandy and cook for a few minutes, stirring well to reduce the sauce a little so it thickens.

To serve, place the salmon on a warmed plate, top with the sauce, and garnish with strips of roasted red pepper.

Baked Salmon Parcels

SERVES 4

Preheat oven to 400 degrees

4 salmon fillets, about 7 oz each

1 medium onion, peeled and thinly sliced

1 medium leek, white part only, julienned

1 large head of fennel

4 oz butter

1/2 cup white wine

Remove and discard the tough outer layer of the fennel. Slice the fennel thinly and sauté with the onion and leek in butter until the onion is translucent.

Measure 4 pieces of aluminum foil about 8" square. Place a salmon fillet on each square. Top each fillet with a quarter of the vegetable mixture and sprinkle with white wine. Wrap each fillet up securely, making sure enough space is left between the foil and salmon to allow steam to rise. Also make sure the edges of the foil are sealed tightly so that none of the cooking liquid leaks out during baking.

Place the foil packages on a cookie sheet and bake for 12 to 15 minutes at 400 degrees. When cooked, open each foil package carefully and slide the contents onto individual serving plates. Serve immediately, garnished with fresh parsley.

Poached Salmon with Tomato, Fresh Thyme & Crème Fraiche

As served by Bill Conway, chef-owner of the Captain Linnell House in Orleans.

SERVES 4

4 fillets of Atlantic salmon, 4-6 oz each

1 tablespoon butter

1 tablespoon chopped shallots

1 cup blanched, deseeded and diced tomatoes

2 teaspoons fresh chopped thyme

1/4 cup Pernod

1 cup crème fraiche

salt and pepper to taste

COURT BOUILLON:

1/2 cup white wine vinegar

2 stalks celery, chopped

1 carrot, chopped

1 onion, peeled and chopped

1 bay leaf

1 cup white wine

2 quarts water

If necessary, skin and bone the salmon. Combine all ingredients for the court bouillon in a large pot and bring to a boil. Lower to a simmer and poach the salmon gently in this liquid for 8 to 10 minutes.

Melt a tablespoon of butter in a sauce pot. Add the chopped shallots and sauté for a minute or so. Stir in the tomatoes and fresh thyme. Add the Pernod and flambé—heat the pan until the Pernod is hot and then tip the pan so the Pernod catches fire. Remove from the heat when the alcohol has burned off. Stir in a cup of crème fraiche and reduce the sauce over medium heat until it thickens. Season to taste with salt and pepper.

To serve, place the poached salmon on heated plates and spoon sauce generously over the fish. Garnish with sprigs of fresh thyme.

NOTE: If crème fraiche is unavailable, you may make it by combining one quart of heavy cream with one cup of buttermilk. Mix well and keep in a warm place for 4 to 6 hours, and then refrigerate, where the mixture will thicken. Crème fraiche also makes a delicious alternative to yogurt or heavy cream on fresh fruit or pies.

Oldest known photo of the Captain Linnell House in Orleans, taken in 1850, showing Rebecca, widow of Captain Ebenezer Harding Linnell, with her three daughters: Helen, Florentina, and Abigail.
The Captain Linnell House was built in 1840 .

Grilled Salmon with Maple Balsamic Glaze

SERVES 4

4 salmon steaks or fillets, 5 or 6 oz each

1/4 cup grapefruit or orange juice

1/4 cup maple syrup

3 tablespoons balsamic vinegar

2 cloves garlic, minced

1 tablespoon olive oil

Light a charcoal fire and make sure the grate is clean. Season the salmon steaks or fillets with salt and pepper and place in a shallow pan or bowl. Combine juice, maple syrup, balsamic vinegar, and garlic in a small sauté pan. Bring to a boil and cook for 5 or 6 minutes, stirring so the ingredients are well blended, and then add the oil. Pour over the salmon and let it marinate in the glaze for at least half an hour. When the fire is hot, grill the salmon for 5 minutes on each side, or until done, brushing frequently with the glaze.

Wychmere Harbor, Harwich, c. 1920   POSTCARD COURTESY OF NOEL W. BEYLE

Baked Salmon Wrapped in Grape Leaves

SERVES 6

Preheat oven to 400 degrees

6 salmon fillets with skin and any bones removed

1 cup extra virgin olive oil

1/4 cup fresh lemon juice

1/4 teaspoon cayenne pepper

2 tablespoons chopped fresh coriander

20 grape leaves

In a bowl combine the olive oil, lemon juice, cayenne pepper, and coriander. Place the salmon in a shallow dish. Pour the marinade over the salmon and refrigerate for 10 or 12 hours, turning occasionally.

In the spring you may use fresh grape leaves that have just unfurled, otherwise use canned. Lay 2 or 3 grape leaves on a flat surface, slightly overlapping, and remove the stems.

Place one salmon fillet in the center, top with a tablespoon of marinade, and fold the leaves over the salmon to cover completely. Turn the package upside down so the loose ends are underneath. Wrap the other fillets in the same manner and arrange the salmon packages in a baking pan. Bake the salmon at 400 degrees for 12 or 15 minutes, depending on the thickness of the fillets. Serve with a tomato, cucumber, and mint salad and yogurt dressing.

Gravlax

This traditional Scandinavian recipe comes from Astrid Berg of Pepe's Wharf seafood restaurant in Provincetown.

SERVES 4
AS AN
APPETIZER

1 large fillet of fresh salmon

1/2 cup kosher salt

2 tablespoons sugar

1/4 cup cognac or vodka

1/4 cup chopped fresh dill

1/2 red onion, thinly sliced

1 tablespoon capers

1/4 cup Dijon mustard

1/4 cup mayonnaise or whipped cream

pumpernickel bread

Mix the salt and sugar together. Arrange the fillet of salmon on a large piece of plastic wrap placed on top of a piece of aluminum foil. Rub the salt/sugar mixture all over the salmon, on top and underneath. Enclose the fillet tightly in plastic wrap and place in the refrigerator for at least 6 hours or overnight.

After the time has elapsed, uncover the salmon and rinse off any salt that hasn't been absorbed. Rub some cognac or vodka all over the salmon and cover the fish with chopped fresh dill. Rewrap the salmon well in plastic wrap and foil and place in the refrigerator on a tray with another tray on top, weighted with at least 5 lbs, to press the salmon and tighten the meat. Leave overnight.

When ready, unwrap the salmon and slice thinly on the bias. Serve with a mustard sauce made with half Dijon mustard and half mayonnaise or whipped cream. Garnish with fresh dill, thin slices of red onion and capers, and serve with pumpernickel bread.

Spicy Salmon Cakes

A perfect recipe for using up any leftover cooked salmon.

1 or 2 cups cooked salmon

1 or 2 cups mashed potatoes

1/2 cup minced onion or scallions

1/4 cup fresh chopped parsley

1/2 teaspoon peeled, finely-minced fresh ginger

1 teaspoon minced or crushed garlic

1 teaspoon Dijon mustard

2 eggs, beaten

1/2 cup white bread crumbs

salt and pepper to taste

1/2 cup olive oil

Flake the salmon and mix with the mashed potatoes. Add the onion, parsley, ginger, garlic, mustard, salt and pepper. Mix everything together with the beaten eggs and add about half a cup of bread crumbs so the mixture is stiff and not too moist. Shape into small cakes, roll in bread crumbs, and leave to dry on a rack for about 15 to 30 minutes.

Heat the olive oil in a large skillet over medium-high heat. Place as many cakes in the pan as will fit, and turn the heat to high. Cook until browned on both sides, removing the pan from the heat when necessary so the cakes brown but do not burn. You may need to do this in several batches. Drain on paper towels before serving. These cakes may also be broiled or grilled, if you prefer. Serve with lemon wedges.

Smoked Salmon Chowder

An unusual version of a traditional chowder from Donna Aliperti,
chef/owner of the renowned Front Street Restaurant in Provincetown.

SERVES 4

1 lb smoked salmon, diced

1 lb white potatoes, peeled and diced

1 medium onion, minced

4 ribs celery, minced

1/4 cup olive oil

4 tablespoons clarified butter

1 teaspoon fresh thyme,
   or 1/2 teaspoon dried thyme

2 cups clam juice

2 cups half-and-half

2 tablespoons flour

2 tablespoons water

Sauté the onions and celery in olive oil and butter until transparent. Add potatoes and clam juice. Simmer until potatoes are tender, about 15 or 20 minutes. Add thyme, salmon, and half-and-half. Bring to a low simmer. Mix 2 tablespoons of flour with 2 tablespoons of water to make a watery paste and add slowly to the simmering soup to thicken. Add enough to attain desired thickness. Add salt and pepper to taste and continue cooking for 3 to 4 minutes to remove floury taste. Serve in soup plates garnished with a sprinkling of chopped parsley.

The "Paulo Marc" heading home to Provincetown with a good catch.

PHOTO: VINCENT GUADAZNO

Index

Book Order Form

Quantity	Title	Price	Total
	The Cape Cod Fish & Seafood Cookbook by Gillian Drake	$14.95	
	Traditional Portuguese Recipes from Provincetown by Mary Alice Cook Born in Alhoa, Portugal, in 1914, Mary Alice Cook shares over 70 of her family recipes, plus a memoir of Provincetown. With many historic photos. Paperback, 88 pages.	$9.50	
	A Taste of Cape Cod by Gillian Drake A guide to 16 of Cape Cod's finest restaurants, plus more than 100 of their most popular recipes. Paperback, color cover, 96 pages.	$8.50	
	A Taste of Provincetown by Gillian Drake A guide to 15 of Provincetown's finest restaurants, plus more than 100 of their most popular recipes. Paperback, color cover, 96 pages.	$8.50	
	The Complete Guide to Provincetown by Gillian Drake 15 chapters including history, art colony, national seashore, dining and lodging, plus maps and many photos. Paperback, color cover, 148 pages.	$10.95	
	A Guide to the Common Birds of Cape Cod by Peter Trull By Cape Cod's well-known naturalist, this book helps you identify over 120 of the Cape's most common species. Paperback, 72 pages, full-color cover, black and white illustrations.	$9.50	
	Billy's Bird-day by Peter Trull A children's book by Cape Cod's well-known naturalist, this is a cautionary tale about the fragile balance of nature, played out on Cape Cod's sandy beaches. Includes tern field guide and full-color illustrations. Ages 6-11. 32 pages, hard-bound with dust jacket in full color.	$14.95	

SUB-TOTAL	
MASS. RESIDENTS ADD 5% MASS TAX	
SHIPPING*	
TOTAL	

*SHIPPING:
BOOK RATE–$2.00 FOR FIRST BOOK;
$1.25 FOR EACH ADDITIONAL BOOK.
PRIORITY MAIL–$3.00 PER BOOK

SEND CHECK AND MAILING ADDRESS TO:
Shank Painter Publishing
P. O. Box 2001 • Provincetown • MA 02657